About the Author

The Fairy Bikers comprises two people, namely Liz Atkinson and Tina Oxley. Both Yorkshire born and bred but with completely different upbringings and opposite characters. This is their first book on their mid-life crisis adventures on motorbikes.

Lipstick and Leathers

Fairy Bikers

Lipstick and Leathers

Olympia Publishers
London

www.olympiapublishers.com
OLYMPIA PAPERBACK EDITION

A CIP catalogue record for this title is
available from the British Library.

ISBN: 978-1-80074-418-9

First Published in 2022

Olympia Publishers
Tallis House
2 Tallis Street
London
EC4Y 0AB

Printed in Great Britain

Dedication

We would like to dedicate this book to all those who have
suffered with breast cancer, your strength inspires us.

Acknowledgements

We wish to thank the following, without whom none of this would have happened. Firstly, our families, for putting up with us over two years of neglect and our sponsors, many of which donated raffle prizes so that we could get a good start for our fundraising. Others helped with advertising, printing, advice, etc. – who have all been amazing

Breakthrough Breast Cancer
Calverts Carpets Ltd, Thirsk
DialAFlight, Gary and Scott'
Teasdale Motorcycles, Thirsk
Dyno Centre, Northallerton
Shine Valet, Thirsk
Braithwaites Nursery, Bedale
Leeds Harley-Davidson
Rathergood Radio, Darlington
BBC Radio York
Lady Motorcyclist magazine
The Northern Echo, Darlington
Tim, Lost Adventures
Eagle Riders, LA
Croft Circuit, Darlington
Isle of Man TT
Strikes Garden Centre, Northallerton
Weardale Racing
CGR Tattoo, Ripon
ETS Services Ltd, Richmond
M-Kayz Hair Salon, Pontefract
L'Oreal
Home Shop, Bedale
Red Torpedo
Black Sheep Brewery, Masham
Tesco, Northallerton
Marshall Fitness, Ripon
Keith Lemon
Ride Magazine
Simply Dutch, Leeming Bar
Lookers VW, Northallerton

Sainsbury's, Northallerton
NatWest Bank, Thirsk
Busby Stoop Garage, Thirsk
Alpha, Catterick
Sadlers Garage, Catterick
BP Tyre & Exhaust, Colburn
Bikewise
Hamish Rieck

Chapter 1
Background

Suddenly, Tina grabbed Liz's arm and pulled her onto the ground behind a large gravestone.

"What the fuck did you do that for?" said Liz. "I am already wet and now I am dirty, too."

"Shhhh!" said Tina.

Liz looked at her, completely confused and dazed.

"Look over there, by that black car," Tina said.

When she diverted her eyes towards the car, there was a man hovering around it, looking very suspicious, wearing a rucksack, and he looked like he had a gun, too.

"This is scary," said Tina.

"How the hell can we get to our car now?" Liz hissed.

Not knowing what to do, they stayed glued to their spot. There was no one else in sight and they couldn't get to their car without showing themselves to the man with the gun, as well as the black car and its occupants.

This is the story of how it all started.

Liz and Tina first met at a bike meet around five years before their trip and hit it off immediately.

Although they had completely different backgrounds, and were also the complete opposites, their love of biking moulded them together in a way most people couldn't understand. Liz was an accountant and Tina was a cleaner – what a combination!

Before their epic trip they had two prior adventures, with trips to the Isle of Man TT races, and nothing ever seemed to be straightforward where Tina was involved. She somehow always attracted trouble.

Liz was the calm, non-confrontational, and sensible one. Tina was the complete opposite and was always the first one to create issues. Therefore, Liz seemed to spend most of her time off the bike trying to keep control of her and all the situations they ended up in.

Their first trip to the TT was to be with two other girls. They ended up with four tickets for three of them, so they needed to find a fourth person to sell the ticket to, preferably a female.

Liz went onto one of the bike forums she was a member of and advertised the ticket, stating they would prefer to sell to a female as the trip was to be with three other girls. Within a day, Liz got a reply from a male biker in the North East saying that his wife would love to go and would they consider selling to her, so sell the ticket they did.

A week later she came to Liz's house and met the other girls. They all seemed to get on well and were all excited about their trip. Only one of them had been there before so could give advice on where to watch, etc.

The other people involved in this story have had their names changed, so let's call them Jane and Maggie.

Jane and Maggie had the same bikes, so Maggie decided to get her bike painted a different colour before their trip. Her husband spent many painstaking hours painting her bike pink (yes, PINK!).

Well that would be different.

They had two sets of tickets for ten nights each. The first

two tickets were due to leave five days before the other two, so they would all have five nights together and the other two would have five nights after. The tickets sell so fast, they were unable to get four to travel together.

Liz and Maggie were the first two to head off to Heysham for an early morning sailing. They set off in the daylight and ended up there at night, so had a few hours to kill before their ferry left at two-fifteen a.m.

They arrived into Douglas still in the dark and had to find their way to the camp site in Peel, then get their tent up. It had been a long night.

All went smoothly for a few days, and the weather was glorious, so they went to watch the practise runs and had plenty of time for sunbathing next to their tent. Until Tina and Jane turned up.

Tina and Jane fell out constantly and bickered over putting their tent up, and everything else, for the whole week. This gradually got worse as they had to share a tent too.

As Jane had been to the island a few times before, she said she knew all the good places to watch the racing from. As the others were novices to this, they readily agreed to follow on.

It turned out that this place was somewhere on the mountain called Cronk-y-Voddy. They got there early to get their place and settled in. What they didn't realise was that there were no toilets there and they were going to be stuck there for twelve hours.

There was a butty van about two fields walk away, so Liz and Tina got voted to go and find some food and drinks. A long hike later, in bike boots, they arrived at the van to end up in a long queue; as it was the only food source in sight. Not much was left, as Liz was a vegetarian, only a packet of crisps was on offer. The others managed to get a sandwich out of it and some drinks, this was all they were going to eat and drink all day.

Unfortunately, there was an accident somewhere on the track and, as they were inside the track, the roads were closed and there was no way of getting back to Peel.

There were no toilets, and not many hedges that were private, and they were all desperate for a wee, so they were trying to hold on, but the urges were too strong and one by one they all had to use the hedge. Of course, Tina had to find the nettle patch and sting her bum, this only happens to Tina.

After twelve hours stuck in the field, they found the roads being opened, and, with a whoop of delight, they were on their bikes and back to the site. By this time, it was about nine-thirty p.m. and Liz and Tina swore never to listen to Jane's wonderful ideas again; the lesson was learnt – always watch from the outside of the track so you can move about.

On the last night, they all decided they would have a night out in Douglas. As they would be having a drink, they chose to get the bus in. The bus turned out to be a double decker so, of course, they all ran straight up to the top. The bus had quite a few stops on the way to Douglas and one of them was outside a pub. At this point, Jane and Maggie decided they would lift their tops up and flash themselves at the group of lads hanging around outside. This almost caused a riot as the group surged towards the bus, to the horror of the bus driver.

Earlier on, as Tina gets travel sick, she couldn't cope with the movement of the bus so had gone downstairs with Liz following, much to the moaning of the other two, so they missed the events upstairs. They wondered what all the noise was about and were horrified when they found out later just what had happened. Well, this was going to be an interesting night.

After walking around Douglas and watching some of the entertainment, they ended up in a hotel bar as it seemed quite lively, with the music blaring out onto the street. They managed to locate a table and got themselves comfy with their drinks when the karaoke started. As Jane had already had a few drinks and was not used to drinking, she was straight up there to give it her all, much to the embarrassment of the others, who dragged her off as her singing was so bad.

On the next table was a group of guys who seemed quite surprised to meet a group of lady bikers on their own, so they all got chatting.

This all went very well until it got to midnight and Liz realised that all the taxis had stopped running. They had to get ten miles back to Peel. Oh shit, this was going to be a long walk then.

One of the men in the group offered up the services of one of their mates, who had not been drinking and who had a transit van. This was slightly more preferable to a long walk but being rolled around in a van was still slightly worrying, especially with Tina's travel sickness.

Eventually, they agreed as they had no choice. What were they thinking of, getting into a van with a bunch of guys they had only just met, but then they had Tina, their pocket rocket, to protect them and no one would argue with her!

They all rolled into the back of the van and Liz and Tina noticed that Maggie seemed to be glued to the side of one of the men (let's call him Pete). They thought it was strange as both of them were married and they seemed to be getting quite cosy, but then everyone had been drinking so they thought it was just harmless fun. Wrong!!

The journey back to the tent was difficult, to say the least. Tina kept wanting to be sick, so everyone tried to keep their distance from her, which was slightly difficult when there was eight people stuffed into the back of a transit van.

At last they made it back in one piece to the camp site, slightly worse for wear and with a hangover to look forward to in the morning, which was the day Liz and Maggie were leaving for home.

Apparently, these guys were booked on the same ferry back to Heysham as Liz and Maggie (Tina and Jane still had another five days to go), although two of the guys had to make a court appearance that morning. They had been caught riding the wrong way over the mountain, as this is a one-way system during the TT, so they were not sure they would be allowed off the island. It would depend on whether they could pay their fine.

Liz and Maggie managed to get their tent packed up and got onto the ferry on time, wondering what had happened to the guys that morning. All was to be revealed as they made it onto the ferry, announcing that they had been hit with a two thousand pound fine each, which they had to pay to get their ferry tickets back.

They all sat together for the journey, but Maggie and Pete kept disappearing, much to the hilarity of everyone in the group. They said they were just going outside for some air and a walk, but it appeared something more was transpiring.

When they all disembarked, Maggie and Pete were seen snogging away.

"This is weird," thought Liz, wondering what was going on.

All was quiet after they settled down at home, until Tina got home five days later and rang Liz to relay the events that had happened after Liz had left.

The day after Liz and Maggie had left brought heavy rain and storms to the island, so they were evacuated from the campsite and managed to find accommodation with one of the islanders for one night until they got booked into a hotel.

They booked into their hotel the next morning, into a twin room, still bickering. The bickering continued until they got home. This flared up when they got off the ferry and Tina's foot slipped whilst she was waiting for Jane to finish her cigarette, so she shouted to her for help. Jane ignored her, so Tina had to let her bike drop to the ground. By this time Tina was like a raging bull and tore a strip off Jane, who then eventually helped her get the bike upright.

Needless to say, the fab four were no more.

Their second trip to the TT was even more eventful. It was the following year and Tina had been the organiser (first time ever). She had bought four tickets before she had left the island the previous year.

She had intended on going back with her husband and two of their friends, but it turned out that none of them could go, so she was left with three spare tickets.

On hearing that Tina had got her tickets for the following year, Liz bought one direct from the ferry company but could only get one for five nights. But that would do quite nicely.

Tina sold the first one to a guy called Dave who had been wanting to go for ages in his car, so he managed to change his ticket from a bike one to a car one. Then she had to find two more people who wanted to buy the other tickets from her, maybe not to travel with them as they were a bit nervous after the last trip and the issues that arose from travelling with others.

Tina spoke to a few people she knew and one of her friends said his wife was interested.

"Not again," she thought, but sold them to a girl called Anne who wanted to bring her friend with her.

Great, another foursome, let's hope this time they can all get on!

It turned out that the fourth person was a guy. Nothing wrong with that, they thought (at first).

They had all arranged to meet at Tina's house for the ride to the ferry at Liverpool. Liz was there early as usual; Tina wasn't ready, as usual, and there was no sign of Anne. After about an hour, Anne turned up and by then it was raining quite hard. Liz and Tina weren't happy as they could have had an hour riding before the rain came but, hey-ho, these things happen. Anne announced that her friend, let's call him Mick, still hadn't left home, so he would catch them up. Apparently, he realised that the MOT had run out on his bike that morning, so he had to book it in quick. And then, as he tried to leave home, it turned out that his bike was too wide for his gate with all the panniers on, so he had to unpack it and then repack before he could even get to the garage. None of this boded well. He also lived another thirty miles further north, so had a lot of catching up to do.

The three girls set off and plodded on through the rain. Feeling cold and wet, they found somewhere to stop for lunch. There was a Little Chef on the way, and they thought that would do – any opportunity to take off their waterproofs and dry out.

Once they were warmed up and fed, they then had the task

of putting wet waterproofs back on, not a task relished by any biker, then off they went towards Liverpool.

The rain eventually subsided and left a miserable, grey day behind it but that was a relief compared to riding in the rain.

Once they got into Liverpool, they had the task of keeping together and finding the ferry terminal. Luckily for them it was well signposted and there were plenty of other bikers loaded up, so they figured they must be going to the same place. The traffic had built up so they tried to filter through it, forgetting they had panniers on so the bikes were wider than they were used to. This caused a few scary moments and no doubt it did for some of the car drivers, too.

They rolled up into the queue to get onto the ferry and there was still no sign of Mick, so Anne decided to text him and tell him to ring when he got there as Tina had his ticket.

Following everyone else, they gingerly rode onto the ferry and duly lined up their bikes where they were directed. The ferry staff gave them a strap and a pad to use to fasten their bikes down. Immediately, they played the helpless females and, with a bit of flattery, persuaded the ferry staff to do it for them. Feeling smug, they headed up to the passenger deck to find a comfy spot.

Just as they were wondering where Mick had got to, he rang Anne to say he had arrived. She went down to meet him with his ticket so he could get on board. This was to be the first time Liz and Tina had met him when he came upstairs with Anne.

They all got settled down in their seats, Anne and Mick in the two seats in front of Liz and Tina.

Part of the way through the crossing, Mick turned round

and offered Liz and Tina some condoms out of his packet. They were perplexed and thought he was joking but, oh no, it turned out he was serious. They would soon realise what was going on.

After a fairly smooth crossing, the ferry had arrived at Douglas harbour. Everyone was up and rushing downstairs to the car deck to be the first back to their bikes and to get ready for rolling off the ferry.

There were so many bikes, they couldn't remember where they had left theirs and they were packed in so tight, they could barely get through between the rows of bikes to look. Fortunately, Anne was quite tall so she could scan the deck to spot the bikes. Off they went, pushing and shoving to reach them, then they had to unstrap them and get ready to offload when it was their turn.

They spotted where Mick had parked. As it wasn't too far away from them he was going to join up with them when they rode off the ferry. It was very slippery underfoot and took some careful, gentle movements to set off, and then there was a U-turn ahead of them to be able to face the other way to ride off. They were terrified of dropping their bikes. Being girls, they did not want to show themselves up on a male-dominated ferry, they tiptoed and pushed their bikes, rode extremely slowly, and crept along. Mick tagged on behind them and, as he went round the U-turn, he dropped his bike straight onto the deck.

This amused the girls no end. Typical bloke showing off, they thought, and look where it got him. A few bikers rushed to help him lift the loaded bike up so that he could get off, the girls just left him to catch up with them on land.

By this time it was around nine-thirty p.m. and they still

had to ride ten miles to the campsite at Peel.

Liz and Tina had bought a new tent with two bedrooms in it and, due to the fact that it was quite heavy (and large), they decided to pack it up, along with their bedding and anything they could get into the box, and send it by courier to the campsite. They were very pleased with themselves for coming up with this plan and the campsite office was going to keep it until they arrived.

It was just after ten p.m. when they eventually got themselves to the site, they went straight to the office to collect their tent, only to find that it had closed at ten p.m. and was not open until the next morning. They had nowhere to sleep all night – disaster.

Anne and Mick had taken a small tent each, so it was decided that they would all sleep in the larger of the two tents, which had a small bedroom at each end and a gap down the middle with a divider. Wondering how this was going to work, Liz and Tina were directed into one side, which was very cosy. Liz had to sleep next to Tina, again!

They thought that Mick would be sleeping in the smaller tent on his own and Anne would be in the same tent as them, but no, that was not to be.

Liz and Tina thought it was odd that the other two seemed to be quite happy to sleep next to each other. After all, Anne was married to Tina's friend.

As Liz was exhausted, she put her earplugs in and immediately fell into a deep sleep, where she stayed until morning. Her first thought was yippee, she can collect their tent.

Once Tina realised Liz had woken up, she asked her if she had had a good night's sleep.

"Oh yes, great," replied Liz.

Then Tina launched into a tirade about her sleepless night.

Tina said, "I couldn't sleep as I had to listen to those two shagging!"

"What!" said Liz.

"Oh, fuck yes," said Tina.

Oh dear, this was going to be another nightmare in the making.

As they still had their clothes on from the night before, they shot out of the tent and straight to the campsite office to collect their box containing their promised peace.

When they got back to Anne's tent and started pitching theirs, on the next plot, they realised what the smaller tent was for. It was for keeping all their kit in and they had no intention of sleeping in separate tents for the next two weeks.

Tina, not being backward in coming forward, went straight up to Anne to find out what was going on. It turned out that Mick was Anne's 'friend with benefits' and was unknown to her husband. Tina told her she wanted nothing to do with it and refused to lie on her behalf, which caused a few ruffled feathers.

During all this, Dave arrived and parked next to the tents in his car. He soon cottoned on to the situation and was every bit as disgusted as Liz and Tina.

Dave hadn't brought a tent as he was intending to sleep in his car. He had brought a duvet and pillows, etc. so seemed to be quite comfy in there. As he had his car and not his bike, he was itching to have a bike to ride so asked if anyone would mind if he borrowed their bike. All were quiet, until Tina eventually offered hers up.

As Tina's husband had taken the back pegs off before her

trip (as she wouldn't need them), the only way they could both get onto her bike was if Dave took the pegs off Liz's bike and put them onto Tina's, as a temporary measure. Tina ended up going pillion on her own bike for the rest of the trip.

As the days went on, Liz and Tina had to listen to Anne on the phone to her husband every day, telling him she was missing him, whilst sat next to Mick, with their arms round each other. They were getting very sick of it and felt like they had really been taken for a ride. Things could only get better.

Apart from their day out into Douglas to see the Purple Helmets display. Dave would drive and the other four would cram into his car, Tina in the front seat (due to her travel sickness issue), so Liz ended up having to lie down in the back next to Anne and Mick, who proceeded to fondle each other all the way. Liz couldn't wait to get out.

They parked up in Douglas and decided they had time to have a walk around and watch the entertainment, etc. Then, whilst starting to cross the road, Liz and Tina noticed that Anne and Mick seemed to be arguing about something. All of a sudden, Anne sat down on the traffic island with her legs and arms crossed and refused to move until she got her own way, whatever that was.

Tina said, "Sod them, then."

Liz and Dave followed her off the road and into the shopping area, leaving the other two to catch up when they had finished arguing.

Eventually they caught up and things seemed calmer, so they got back into the car and headed up to the showground where the display was to take place. They all bought their tickets, except Dave, who refused to spend any money and said he would sit in his car and try and get in later for free.

Meanwhile, all throughout the show, Anne and Mick kept cuddling up and snogging, so Liz and Tina kept shifting themselves along a bit to keep their distance.

Towards the end of the show, Dave turned up. He had managed to get in free, so he saw the last fifteen minutes. Was it really worth it though?

After the show, they all had to repeat the same journey back to the campsite in Dave's car. That ten miles seemed like forever to Liz.

Back at the tent, the canoodling continued, even through another phone call to her husband.

Liz and Tina were so looking forward to going home.

Liz's ticket was only for five nights, whilst the others had ten nights. Liz was relieved as she was feeling ready to get back home.

The day before Liz was due to leave, Tina begged to go back with her as she said she couldn't stand being there, playing gooseberry to those two. So Liz rang up the ferry company who happily changed her ticket to the following morning, onto the same ferry.

Tina decided she wouldn't tell Anne, so she started packing her stuff up and hid it all under her sleeping bag. They spoke to Dave, who said he would pack up their tent and take it back with him as he lived in Yorkshire; not too far away. It was arranged that they would go and collect it once he got back home. He didn't want to be left with those two either but said he would stay.

As it was Liz's last night, they went to a local pub for a meal and a few drinks, but before they set off, Tina wanted to charge her phone. Rather than leave it in the shower block on charge, Dave said he had a charger under his car bonnet, and she could use that. This was plugged in and the bonnet was closed onto the latch before they went out.

As Liz was due to get up at five a.m. to catch the seven a.m. ferry, she announced that she would head back to the tent a bit earlier than everyone else. Tina said that she was tired and would go back too, as she didn't want anyone to know she was leaving in the morning.

On their way back to the tent, Tina unhooked the car bonnet and got her phone out, then closed it and went into the tent to do her final packing and settle down for the night.

After they had got into their beds, and about half an hour later, they heard a commotion outside their tent. With the walls being quite thin, Tina shouted to Dave outside to find out what was wrong. Well, apparently, he used to leave his car keys in a safe place, so he didn't lose them. His safe place was under his car bonnet and, of course, Tina had closed it.

Well, they tried everything to get those keys out and more and more men on the campsite came along to watch and offer their ideas. In the meantime, Liz and Tina were trying to get some sleep, but this continued on until around one a.m. when someone managed to get under the car and reach them from under the engine. All during this commotion, Dave kept coming into their tent, looking for any items he could use to help him break into the car. As the centre of the tent held all their cooking equipment, etc. he was in and out, getting knives, corkscrews, tin openers, and anything else that looked like it could be useful. All Liz and Tina could hear was the tent being unzipped and rezipped again and again, so, in the end, Tina shouted at him that if she heard that tent zip being opened once more she would come out there and bang his head on the bonnet. Well, that sorted that one out, it was time to get a couple of hours sleep.

At around five a.m., Liz's alarm went off and, not being a morning person, she struggled to get up but knew she had to get a move on. She woke Tina up and the two of them went to the toilet block to get a quick wash and a wee before they got the bikes packed up.

They tried to do all this quietly, as everyone knows, especially them, how thin tent walls are and they didn't want to alert Anne and Mick to Tina's imminent departure without them.

As they were loading up the bikes in the dark, they had to tiptoe around to clip on Tina's panniers quietly and get everything out of the tent.

Once the bikes were loaded up, they then had to push them onto the gravel track that led out of the site. They knew that everyone was expecting one bike to start up but not two, so how to do this... would this be the Great Escape or Mission Impossible?

They would push Tina's bike by stealth so that it was as far away from the tent as they could manage. This proved tricky on gravel and with a loaded bike, so, with their heart in their mouths, they heaved it off the grass and onto the track road. They were going to try and start the bikes at the same time, so that it only sounded like one bike starting—in hindsight, this was a bit of a silly move as anyone can tell it's two bikes.

They got them started and rode off the campsite as quick as they could and went the back way to Douglas, just in case Anne decided to follow them. They knew she wouldn't want to be left behind, as Tina couldn't be seen out at home without her, in case her husband wondered why.

They rode as fast as they could to the ferry port and got checked in. They then sat down with a cuppa and a big sigh that they had done it.

Just as they sat down, Tina's phone rang. It was Anne. She had heard the bikes roar away and had realised what had gone on. She was fuming with Tina as she said she couldn't stay now because she had lost her alibi. Tina told her to stay and enjoy the rest of her trip; and that was that, they thought.

As soon as the announcement came for passengers to ride onto the ferry, they were off as quick as possible. They weren't going to be relieved until the ferry was out at sea.

Thankfully, they made it and had a much more peaceful sailing back than the one going out. The ride home was so much less stressful, too.

By the time they got home, they realised that they had just been stressed most of the time they were away and vowed never to travel in a group of more than two of them again.

Chapter 2
The Beginning

Once upon a time…

OK, maybe that wasn't a great beginning, but where the hell else can this story start.

Two middle-aged, menopausal Yorkshire lasses embarked on a great adventure. It wasn't perfect and it wasn't pretty, but they achieved what everyone that knew them said they couldn't manage. They were Liz and Tina.

It all started whilst they were discussing their bucket list during one of their weekly girlie nights in, as just one of those 'I wish' moments, then they just looked at each other and said, "let's do it!" Neither of them needed any further persuading and the seed of adventure was sown.

It was a lightbulb moment when it all seemed a great idea and, with both being totally impulsive and irrational, there was no stopping them. A dangerous combination!

Their idea was to ride Harley Davidson motorbikes round America, which seemed an adventurous feat to two fairly novice bikers, but they wouldn't be told otherwise and proceeded to forge ahead with their plan.

As Tina had already arranged to visit the NEC bike show, she went under instructions to bring back as much information as possible from the adventure trade stands. She duly brought back a haul of brochures, along with lots of enthusiasm.

After searching through the brochures, they decided that

they would err on the side of caution and not go straight in for a long trip across America. They would just dip their toe in to see how it went before planning a bigger trip. After all, they could always do another one.

The one that caught their eye was to take them to America to ride a Harley Davidson motorbike each from Las Vegas, through Death Valley to San Francisco, then down the Californian coastline and straight into Los Angeles, but could they do it?

The trip would join them up with a small group of like-minded people from all over the world, all staying in the same hotels and all riding together, surely it couldn't be that simple! They didn't realise Tina was on her way. Chaos was about to hit.

The tour they had chosen was through a company called Eagle Riders and was called the 'Wild West II'. The plan was to cover one thousand, one hundred and sixty miles over nine days. Simple!

After looking through the itinerary, it seemed a long way to go for nine days and, after considering the potential jet lag and the travelling, they figured they would find themselves too tired to enjoy it. So why not add a few days on before the trip and a few after? That way they could also see some of the country. Hence, nine days ended up being almost three weeks.

What started as a seed became a forest; something much larger than they had ever done before.

After visiting the Isle of Man TT races for two years in succession, with different groups of people, and having the kind of stories to tell that you just couldn't make up, the idea took hold of writing the story of their adventure and sharing their latest exploits. As if anyone would really be interested...

It soon became apparent to Liz that maybe she had got in too deep, embarking on a trip with Tina, who is like a bull in a China shop. Travelling with her is not for the faint-hearted.

During the planning process, Tina got the devastating news that her mother had been diagnosed with breast cancer, it was April 2014. This then caused a re-think and they decided to change their plans slightly and thought that they could use this trip to raise money for breast cancer and the awareness of it, whilst also having a great time.

After much deliberation, they decided to support Breakthrough Breast Cancer, who have since changed their name to Now Breast Cancer.

It sounds like an amazing holiday of a lifetime but would they do it again? Not unless kidnapping was involved.

Readers beware, this book is not for those with a nervous disposition. Thinking of going on holiday with a friend? Think again!

The itinerary they put together, along with the guided tour itinerary, was:

May 10th: Day One – flight

May 11th: Day Two – Las Vegas

May 12th: Day Three – Grand Canyon

May 13th: Day Four – Las Vegas

May 14th: Day Five – collect bikes from the Eagle Rider base in Las Vegas

May 15th: Day Six – Las Vegas to Mammoth Lakes through Death Valley – three hundred and fifteen miles

May 16th: Day Seven – Mammoth Lakes to Yosemite – one hundred and fifty miles

May 17th: Day Eight – Yosemite to San Francisco – two hundred miles

May 18th: Day Nine – San Francisco

May 19th: Day Ten – San Francisco to Monterey – one hundred and eighteen miles

May 20th: Day Eleven – Monterey to Pismo Beach – one hundred and fifty-two miles

May 21st: Day Twelve – Pismo Beach to Los Angeles – two hundred and twenty-five miles

May 22nd: Day Thirteen – hand back the bikes

May 23rd: Day Fourteen – Hollywood Boulevard

May 24th: Day Fifteen – Universal Studios

May 25th: Day Sixteen – San Diego

May 26th: Day Seventeen – Warner Bros

May 27th: Day Eighteen – Flight home

May 28th: Day Nineteen – Arrive in Heathrow and head for home.

Chapter 3
The Planning

Twelve to eighteen months to take off (December 2013 to May 2014).

Diary of events:

December 2013

Shortly after Tina's visit to the bike show, they were contacted by a guy called 'Tim', who was the UK agent. He was very informative and answered all their ridiculous questions, including 'how much girlie stuff can we fit on a bike?' (By the way, the answer was 'very little'). He managed to reply to everything without laughing. He must have wondered what they were going to turn up with; it was going to be a challenge to pack light.

They jumped straight in and booked their places for September 2014. As the booking was made just before Christmas, they spent the whole festive period plotting and scheming how they were going to approach this adventure and where to start. They did some research and couldn't find any stories on any similar trips made by girlie bikers to inspire them, so they decided to write their own. As nothing is ever straightforward when Tina is involved, it was inevitable that this trip would follow suit.

Forging ahead at top speed, they headed off to check out the bikes on offer at the Harley Davidson dealership, as they had to confirm to Tim which bikes they wanted and, having never ridden a Harley, they thought they could sit on a few and see which one felt the most comfortable. It wasn't going to be easy to choose a bike to travel all those miles when you can only sit on one and not get the chance to test ride it.

After explaining their plans, the salesmen were kind enough to let them sit on a number of bikes. Therein discovering the first obstacle – Tina was too short for all the bikes in the shop!

They now entered panic mode and the trip was looking risky.

The salesman appeared slightly worried when she sat on a bike and couldn't put her feet on the floor, so had balanced it on her toes. To avoid the domino effect rippling through the showroom of brand-new Harley bikes, he shot over and tried to divert them to the coffee machine and a table of brochures to distract them (looking a bit nervous).

After successfully negotiating them out of harm's way, he then felt more relaxed to explain about an ultra-low version of the bike she wanted and suggested they look into that possibility. Unfortunately, they didn't have one at their site (strangely enough), but Tina and Liz did leave armed with brochures and the suggestion that they try another Harley shop (did that mean they were barred?).

Another discussion was going to have to be made with tolerant Tim! Yet again, he took it all in his stride and assured them that Tina's height wouldn't be a problem.

As they were approaching everything at breakneck speed, and without a thought for anyone else in their quest for adventure, they were suddenly halted in their tracks by the very sensible Darran (Tina's husband).

Bump! Back to reality…

"Have you thought how much this trip was going to cost?" He asked. "And exactly how are you going to save all that before September?"

Err, of course they had thought of that, was their reply (that thought actually didn't come into it), so a compromise was needed. the best they could offer was a postponement to the following May, giving them plenty of saving time and the all-important planning time. They must learn to gain some patience.

Back to tolerant Tim! After explaining the situation, he said he could book them on to the May 2015 trip. Although he didn't have the dates yet they didn't care, they just wanted in!

Finally, the deposit of two hundred and fifty pounds each was paid – on the third of January 2014 – yippee, it was all systems go and the excitement started to build.

There was not much more that could be done at this stage, at least not until the actual trip dates were confirmed, so they spent their time researching what else they could get up to.

They planned to arrive a few days earlier and leave a few days after the end of the trip and take the opportunity to take in the sights, but what to do with that time? So much to see.

After a short period of time spent on the internet, they realised they just had to visit the Grand Canyon. There were so many trips on offer, so they started narrowing them down. The coach trip had to get scrubbed off the list, due to Tna's travel sickness issues (sick bags was not an option to pack), and five hours each way on a coach sounded like a complete waste of valuable holiday time. They decided to book onto a fixed-wing plane as the helicopter looked too scary. Maybe they would just sleep on this decision for a bit.

January 2014

After the decision to record their trip, the next step was to find a way to do it. Therefore, after some research (thank goodness for the internet), they downloaded some software that enabled them to add text onto PC and mobile whenever they wanted. Feeling very positive, they started to record everything that happened online and in notebooks.

At one of their weekly meets for supper, their next bright idea was to set up a blog (they had heard of these, so surely it coudn't be that difficult as everyone does it, don't they?). Only, with no idea where to start, the first problem was to find out what a blog was. After some internet research, they managed to learn the basics and set one up. After a few frustrating hours, the two technophobes couldn't get any pictures uploaded so happily gave up this stupid idea. So, this blank blog will be somewhere in the cloud without an owner and there it will stay!

February 2014

The invoice and receipts were received for the deposit, but still no news on dates yet, which were due out the following week. Then they would have to make their choice – not more decisions.

At the end of the month, the dates were out so it was decided to go for the first tour of the year, starting on the fourteenth of May, as they couldn't wait any longer. Fingers crossed, they waited for confirmation.

March 2014

They got the confirmation of the dates and they had got the first tour of the year. The trip was to start on the fourteenth of May 2015, yippee, they couldn't wait! Not much could be done until the flights had been released and they seemed to be eleven months in advance. More waiting.

In the meantime they pondered on how they could save, as the costs were spiralling with all their plans. They came to the conclusion that car boot sales would be a good start as they both had lots of surplus stuff at home that needed clearing out. So they kept busy collecting lots of items for a run of car boot sales to raise money to kit them out for their trip. Every suitably dry Sunday afternoon for the foreseeable future would be spent selling their wares, but it would all be worth it!

April 2014

Their first car boot sale was held in Ripon, North Yorkshire – this was chosen due to the timings, as it was an afternoon sale so no early starts! The car was duly loaded up and they set off to join the sellers' queue. Whilst in the queue, they passed the time by trying to decide on a name to use, rather than just use their own. Based on a list of inspiring ideas they had saved up over the last few weeks, the name that was chosen just jumped out at them. Hence, the Fairy Bikers were born.

After eventually getting in, they set up two tables and got to work setting up their stall. Unfortunately, it was a very windy day so most of the time was spent chasing around trying to recover their wares from the surrounding area. This also limited the amount of items that could be displayed, so they returned home after two hours with a full car load – although they still made a profit of fifty-eight pounds and ninety-six pence to go into their pot. Not great, you might think, but for them every penny was going to count.

The second car boot sale was at same place, but a bit less windy. Although they had to cope with a couple of showers and with trying to wrestle with the clothes rail, which fell over every time someone touched any item of clothing on it, much to their embarrassment. A better day than last week as they took one hundred and ten pounds and nine pence, so the travel pot was starting to grow!

As they still brought a carload of items back, they hoped to chance their luck again the following week; depending on the weather. This was to become a weekly event and took up most of their weekends for the summer months, but needs must.

Another week sorting junk out, but they still didn't seem to have any shortage at home, which was quite disconcerting. Where did it all come from and where to store it? Luckily, Darren came to the rescue and offered them one of his sheds to store it all. This was so much easier, having a dedicated space.

The third car boot sale. Over a cuppa at Tina's house before the weekly trip, they entertained themselves by peering through her kitchen window, watching Darran hard at work loading the car (until he realised he had been conned into it and promptly stopped). They then finished the job and set off for the third round of fundraising at the usual venue, with high hopes of matching last week's profits.

After patiently waiting in the queue and passing the time emptying the flasks (that were supposed to last all day), they got through and parked up about a car length away from the camper van next to them. Only to be shooed further away by the older lady, who had parked up before them. They were a bit shocked at the stall possessiveness shown, but never mind, it wasn't going to stop them completing their mission.

They had now got a good routine going of setting up, so it didn't take them long. Then the stampede started when the buyers were let in, so it was all hands on deck for a while.

More cups of tea and coffee later they had their picnic, kindly made up by Tina (as both were on diets – more salad!). Rain stopped play again, but at least they managed a couple of hours first! This week's profit was sixty-six pounds and eighty pence, so better than expected – the result was two happy fairy bikers.

The end of April was chaotic, after their decision to use the opportunity of their trip to raise money for Breakthrough Breast Cancer and to ask for sponsors to support them to ride the one thousand, one hundred and sixty miles.

They got together one evening and drafted up a plan of action. Firstly, they needed to contact the charity and make sure they were happy with all the plans – this went great, and they soon established a contact there who was extremely helpful. The next problem was having to use the internet to promote it – this was going to be tricky.

Setting up the Just Giving account wasn't too difficult, even for two technophobes, and was just within their capabilities. The big problems started when trying to set up Facebook. This project had now taken all week and was still no further forward. There was no alternative but to hand it over to a young person who was more technologically advanced (not difficult) – namely Liz's daughter. There was still a Twitter account to set up as well – it was all very daunting, and they wondered what they had taken on.

May 2014

One year to go!

The start of May kicked off in the usual haphazard way, causing havoc everywhere they go; although not deliberately – it just happens!

On the first Saturday in May they decided to visit the

motorbike shops in Leeds. As Liz had just got a new car, it was decided that they would travel in that to give her the opportunity to do a long run and see how it performed. So she picked up sick bags (and Tina) and headed off down the motorway, with Tina attempting the navigation.

Most of the journey there was just a normal run out, until they hit Leeds city centre, then chaos ensued.

Unfortunately for Liz, Tina's navigation skills were somewhat lacking as they tried to locate Regent Street (where the bike shops are). Tina's idea of giving directions involved pointing to the route to be taken, although that is difficult to follow when driving. So, needless to say, they ended up twice turning into one-way streets, then having to drive down a bus lane to get out of another sticky situation, along with a number of tricky U-turns.

It was at that point that Tina told Liz that, during her motorbike test, she had L and R stickers on her bike mirrors.

"Why would you do that?" asked Liz.

Tina replied, "To remind me which was left and which was right."

"Oh shit," Liz thought, realising what she had taken on.

After a number of near-misses and 'help me' cries from Liz, they eventually arrived in the bike shop's carpark, and no one was more relieved to get there in one piece without any vehicle damage than Liz. Still shaking, she followed Tina into the store.

After a good look around, they spotted some open face helmets, so thought they would try some on to find out which sizes were needed. This was not straightforward for Tina, as it took her so long to take all her hair clips off to try them on and then to put them all back in her hair. Liz gave up and wandered off round the shop on her own.

Eventually they gave up looking for ladies clothing, as there didn't seem to be much there, so went next door to the other bike shop. As soon as they walked in, Liz found the perfect leather jacket. So, after an expensive purchase, they moved the car to a parking area and bought a ticket, then headed off to find a coffee shop.

Of course, they walked in the wrong direction so had to walk back, then further on, to find one – Tina's directions again! They eventually sniffed one out and got themselves fed and watered and some courage built up to get back in the car and find the Harley Davidson shop.

After a few more wrong turns, and trips round the one-way city centre roads (Tina's finger pointing directions again), they found it.

They went in and Tina managed to sit on some bikes, and found one for little people, namely a Superlow Sportster. Breaking news – Tina can reach the floor!

After a chat to the salesman about their plans, he discreetly steered them off the premises. It may, of course, have been a ploy to get rid of them, as they did seem a little nervous when Tina was sitting on the bikes. She is a bit accident prone, or maybe they had been pre-warned.

The journey home was much more uneventful, thank goodness, but when they got about three miles from Tina's home she declared she felt sick. This sent Liz into a panic – she couldn't have someone being sick in her new car! – not wanting to take the risk of her missing the sick bags, she was told to get out of the car and walk home. The threat did seem to abate the sickness for that last few miles, until Liz could drop her off at home and get away safely and car intact.

It may have been relief for Liz, but Tina was ill for the rest of the day and night after being a passenger.

When the bank holiday weekend arrived, they thought they would have another attempt at the car boot sale. Liz arrived at Tina's to find the car all loaded up, but Tina not ready as usual (Tina has no sense of time). Apparently it was thanks to Darran that the car was ready, so at least they got away a bit earlier. They thought they were ahead of themselves and would be quite high up in the queue.

At about halfway there, Liz asked Tina if she had packed everything they needed. Of course, she had no idea what was in the boot. So Liz rang Darran to find out if he had put the duct tape in the car, as the clothes rail kept collapsing. Apparently not. The next plan was to stop in Ripon to pick a roll up until Darran rang back to say that, as they hadn't taken the clothes rail, why did they want duct tape! At this news, Tina did a quick U-turn and headed back, whilst ringing Darran to ask him to bring the clothes rail and they would meet him halfway. This resulted in some colourful language, but he agreed.

They parked up in the pre-arranged meeting place and waited, and waited, and waited. Half an hour later he appeared (although they only lived five miles from the meeting place). Fantastic, they now had their rail so they set off back again and ended up at the end of the queue. But never mind, they could still get in. Although, after unpacking, they discovered that there was a piece of the rail missing. So they had to improvise with what was left, along with the duct tape, which resulted in a very lopsided rail, but it worked for a while! They left with takings of forty-eight pounds and fifty pence.

Chapter 4
The Planning

Six to twelve months to take off (June to November 2014)
July 2014
They spent a lot of time during this month researching flights and ended up with pages of quotes to work through. They didn't realise there were so many travel companies! As they got turned down for contributions to their flights from Virgin Atlantic and British Airways, it looked like they would have to raise all the funds, they expected to fund the trip themselves, but as they were raising money for charity, it would have been nice to have something towards it.
August 2014
The first Sunday in August was forecast for a fine day, so back to car boot sales at the usual venue. This was not very successful and only managed to make three pounds and fifty pence profit!
They had a dress that had been worn once and cost over fifty pounds and they were asking three pounds for it. One lady tried to knock it down to two pounds and fifty pence, then she walked away when they said no to her. Another lady got into a huff when they asked one pound and fifty pence for a brand-new iPad case and wouldn't reduce the price – they did get put off going back there as everyone seemed to want everything for free and were quite disgusted at the behaviour and attitude of some people. They left there with little faith in human nature

and hoping things would improve next time.

They managed to get the flights booked and the Las Vegas hotel. They would be flying from London Gatwick to Las Vegas, and back from Los Angeles to London Heathrow, and would be staying at the Hotel Bellagio. Scott, at DialAFlight, was fantastic and sorted out a great deal (great service and support from him, so massive thanks to him for helping them on their way). It's rare, nowadays, to get good customer service, so it was much appreciated.

Tina was working in a garage by this time and, being the chatty person she is, she had been telling everyone who would listen about their plans. Luckily for her, a member of the press called in for fuel and, after having suffered the verbal effect of Tina's sales pitch, had promised to do a write-up in the local paper (the Northern Echo) – squeals of excitement followed from Tina as her imagination ran away with her as she dreamed of a front page spread. Well, you never know. The local radio station (Rathergood Radio) had also promised to help promote the fundraising.

They then came up with another promotion idea (well, they thought it was fab anyway), so off they went to their local motorbike shop to ask if they would let them hold a Ladies Day, where they could launch the fundraising campaign. Luckily they agreed, so it was to be held at Teasdales Motorcycles in Thirsk, North Yorkshire.

Now the date and location were fixed, they set to planning what they could put on that was a bit different – this took longer than anticipated but progress was made.

Rathergood Radio had agreed to run a story on them and wanted to do a pre-recorded interview, but, as neither of them wanted to do it, one of them had to bite the bullet.

Tina got the short straw to do the radio interview, so that pre-recording went ahead. It was to be played the following day on Rathergood Radio, so fingers crossed she hadn't said anything completely stupid.

The advert went well, and they were very good at making it sound a bit different, so they played the story every hour on the local news.

They approached lots of companies for raffle prizes. In the hope that they get some, they started planning for other things to do. Lots of begging later, they ended up with some stalls for the Ladies Day event, selling lots of girlie stuff like handmade soaps and crafts, etc.

The Facebook page had turned into a bit of a nightmare. Everything that could go wrong did go wrong, so it was duly passed it onto someone younger and cleverer – Liz's daughter – who spent many conversations trying to explain to them how it worked.

They then had a very successful trip to Leeds and managed to secure raffle prizes from Harley Davidson, Get Geared, and J & A Accessories.

The good news was that Keith Lemon had sent a signed photo to put in the raffle, so a big thank you to him. It was great that someone actually bothered to get back to them with something positive for a change, as most celebs they approached were not interested. They also got a signed T-shirt from Guy Martin, which was fantastic.

They started planning the leaflets and logo design, etc. This took a lot longer than anticipated as neither of them were technologically sound. After hours of coming up with different designs, they thought they had the perfect result. That was until it was sent to Liz's daughter to look at, when she promptly redid it and sent it back. They had to admit that it was far superior to their efforts.

It had been a busy month, with all the planning and meetings, but they had managed to secure lots of great prizes for the raffle, as well as some ex and current TT racers to come and chat to people. They had got stalls and food organised, too. Tina managed to get the local printing shop to print five hundred leaflets as their contribution towards the fundraising, which was a fantastic result, so they spent every opportunity going out on the campaign trail to get people to come to the Ladies Day. Luckily the weather had been great, so they had been able to visit the whole area on their bikes and chat to people and hand out leaflets with a lot of positive responses.

September 2014

This month they got themselves into the local papers, and someone told them they were on the local news on the TV – maybe they were having a bit of an impact, or maybe there was nothing newsworthy at the time and they were scraping the barrel.

Tina was still waiting for news on her mum, which was due anytime this month, so everything was crossed for some good news, but at least they felt they were doing something positive to help.

After another lunchtime meeting, Liz gave Tina a list of jobs to do that week – perhaps that wasn't a good plan! Oh well, at least she never came away empty-handed when sent out to beg for raffle prizes. Today she got a pink kettle from one of the Thirsk market stalls and a scarf from another one, a plant stand from Simply Dutch in Leeming Bar, and a plant voucher from Braithwaites Nursery in Aiskew. Not a bad day in all.

Croft Circuit had promised four tickets for a bike race meet in March, that's an amazing prize.

Tina collected more raffle prizes, and they also received a nice T-shirt from the Black Sheep Brewery. Tina also managed to get an advertising banner that was designed and printed by Eye Catching Printers in Richmond.

An email arrived from the Isle of Man TT races asking for the address to send a raffle prize to – fab!

When meeting for lunch one day, Tina broke her car key card, so she had to leave her car engine running the whole time. Although she hadn't realised this until she went back to the car. Luckily, the car was still there. It had been parked in the market square on a busy shopping day, too.

After receiving a note from the Post Office saying there was a parcel to collect, Liz went to collect it and, upon opening it, there was a box from L'Oreal containing three presentation boxes of skincare – amazing prize from them. They were getting so many prizes now and so many positive responses.

Also, a box was received from the Isle of Man TT containing signed caps, posters, etc.

Tina went back to Sainsbury's in Northallerton, and they gave her a bottle of Prosecco for the raffle, and NatWest in Thirsk gave Liz a couple of bottles of wine. The raffle haul was increasing by the day.

Bit of a disaster day at the end of the month as Darran was taken into hospital with severe back problems, so everything came to a temporary halt.

Over the weekend things were looking better. Tina collected the advertising banner, and also collected two bike MOT vouchers and a plant; whilst Liz managed some bike gloves from Dyno Centre and a voucher from Calverts

Carpets.

October 2014

After a mad rush around, they managed to get everything ready for the big event and Darran was discharged from hospital, too – phew.

Saturday 4th October – D Day. Unfortunately, it rained all day so all the bikers that had promised to come down were rained off, although quite a few got the car out. They were very disappointed as they wanted to have a big show of bikes. It was a busy day, though, and luckily the coffee man was there to warm people up, along with the hog roast that Teasdale Motorcycles brought in. There were so many raffle prizes, so a tombola was set up as well. Everyone was overwhelmed with all the prizes that had been given by local businesses.

The event total raised was six hundred and ninety-one pounds and four pence. Not bad for a miserable October day and a good start for the JustGiving page.

Tina's mum was given the all clear after her breast cancer treatment, definitely a celebration there.

The flights were paid for by the end of the month, another step nearer. The next step was to order themselves a USD currency card each, so that they could save up for their spending money. So much choice, but they thought it would be an easier way to save up by loading some onto it every month. By now, they had realised that they needed to budget for this.

After more research into trips, the one they were totally excited about was the trip to Alcatraz. They had chosen the evening tour so they could see it at night. This was definitely going to be one of the highlights and very spooky.

November 2014

The packing lists were all completed, and Tina was sent home with hers. No doubt, it would get lost before the packing started, so Liz made sure there were a few copies. As they had to cover for every eventuality on the bikes and, bearing in mind they were only stopping one night in places, they would be limited for washing.

They had to think of all weather conditions; they would need waterproofs, layers, jackets, helmets, etc. They decided that, as they were allowed to take two cases each onto the flight, they should take advantage of that and take two. There was no way they could get everything into one case anyway. It was decided to get a box each to put all their shopping contents into to keep them separate and safe – they were feeling well organised now.

They met up after work one evening to look at cases. They thought they would invest in some new, good quality cases as they would need to be sturdy. They bought a cabin case each that were the same make, so they were co-ordinated. Tina got a purple one and Liz got the red one, they would be back for the bigger ones later when their budget allowed.

The list was reviewed again, and it seemed to be getting extremely long, and was starting to look expensive, too.

Another shopping trip resulted in a new rucksack each (this was the only luggage they could carry on the bike), and more toiletries, etc. to go into the packing box. Another list was compiled of all the items they would need for the bike tour, which could be bought at the annual motorbike show at the NEC in Birmingham. Lists and lists and lists.

The last Friday in the month proved very busy, getting ready for their trip to the NEC the next day. They packed a bag, and the car was prepared and filled up. Tina had relented to travel with Liz driving (more sick bags were packed).

After an early start to set off down the A1, they ended up at the Travelodge close by to the NEC eventually, no thanks to Tina's navigating. After checking in, they went to find some food, eventually choosing the hotel nearby as there was no other choice without driving again. This proved to be a poor choice as the food wasn't good and it was expensive – disappointing.

Off they went to bed and were looking forward to a good night, but it proved to be the night from hell. Tina had a problem with her restless legs, so was up and down all night. Her legs hurt, then her hands hurt, then she had indigestion. She was putting the light on, looking for her tablets, then she slept on the floor as she was too hot. Then she got a fan from the hotel to cool her down – poor Liz had three weeks of this to face and she was starting to worry.

The next morning, Liz woke Tina up at eight-thirty from her sudden deep sleep – must find breakfast! The hotel did have a breakfast, so at least they could get something to eat before the long day ahead.

After an uneventful drive to the NEC, they got themselves inside and went straight to the Eagle Rider stand to meet Tim for more conversations about the trip. So many questions to ask and it would be good to meet him and chat in person. They were not sure he had previously had many women booking trips on their own before, so he was possibly unprepared for the onslaught of queries.

They came away with two pairs of bike jeans, a plain, white, open face helmet, a pair of boots each, and also lots of earplugs for Liz.

They had another long drive as they were going straight

to Liverpool for the graduation ceremony the following day for Liz's daughter – they couldn't miss this no matter how tired they were. Liz had hardly slept, due to Tina's shenanigans, and had to drive, which seemed to take forever, to get to Liz's daughter's house to spend the next night there.

Chapter 5
The Planning

Three to six months to take off (December 2014 to February 2015)

December 2014

December started with another bad sleep as Liz had to sleep in the same bed with Tina, who was up and down all night again. By the time they got into Liverpool centre, they looked and felt completely wrecked. The day was fantastic, then another long drive home was facing them. They had to stop at the services on the way back as Tina was feeling sick, so was shown the car door and told not to come back until she felt better, which took a while. They eventually got home around eight-thirty p.m. exhausted.

January 2015

As the new year started, the trip seemed so much nearer now that it was only a few months away, exciting times!

They got back on track again with their plans and got carried away. They booked the hotel in Los Angeles for five nights, along with the hotel in Gatwick airport for the night before the flight out and also the airport lounge, too. Still more bookings to do though.

After getting ahead with those, they got on a bit of a roll and also booked a trip to SeaWorld in San Diego and also a VIP Warner Bros tour in LA. They were getting very excited now, as it is getting nearer, but funds were depleting fast. They had managed to use all the car boot sale profits from the previous summer to pay for all the trips. It had seemed hard at the time to give up all those Sundays, but now it seemed worth it and a long way behind them.

Another booking was made for a private transfer from Las Vegas airport to the hotel. They thought they would travel in style and booked a limo – might as well do it properly.

After meeting up for their normal Friday dinner and planning, they decided to book the trip to the Grand Canyon, which was a half-day morning tour with a visit onto the Sky Walk – very scary for those with a fear of heights. Liz was starting to get worried about this one.

February 2015

They plodded on, posting photos along with the itinerary onto Facebook, and then lost some more Likes – obviously some people didn't like the pictures!

The next booking was for the train tickets to London, one way, eleven weeks to go...

Well, the most exciting thing ever happened this month. They got a phone call asking them if they were interested in going on the One Show on Friday if they could get the show together about lady bikers!

Jeez, not much time! Liz spent half the day trying to get in touch with Tina, who rarely answered her phone, to check her availability and get her opinion. She, of course, was ecstatic and desperately wanted to go. The main problem was that they had to turn up on their bikes.

Ride to London in February on their bikes? Not likely! They were keen, but not keen enough to freeze in the process. Tina had the idea of getting hold of a transit van and transporting the bikes down in that, but then there was getting time off work at this short notice – it all seemed to be fading away at this point.

The following day they got the call to say they didn't get onto the show as they had managed to find enough lady bikers from the local area so didn't need them to travel down – gutted!

By the end of the month, they had finally finished paying for the trip – relief!

As most of the bookings and organising had now been done, things were starting to quieten down a bit but it still seemed so far away.

The last year had been a constant round of raising money and organising. So now the planning was almost coming to an end, it was feeling a little weird.

What would they do after this? This remains an unanswered question!

Chapter 6
The Planning

The last three months' panic to take off (March to May 2015)
March 2015

During this month, they tried to keep busy and collected their helmets, both of which had been sign-written exactly the same, but with their names on. They also had the Facebook page and JustGiving page printed on, too. They looked amazing. They were getting even more excited now!

Another interesting thing happened. They were contacted by someone who was setting up a new lady biker magazine and they wanted to do a feature on the trip. Of course they said yes! They put together some photos and some information about what they were doing and got it sent over straightaway. It would be a shame to miss out on this one. Word seemed to travel fast!

Another unexpected cost arose when they discovered that they had to get additional travel insurance to cover them whilst riding the bikes, as standard travel insurance only covers them to ride up to a 125cc bike – nowhere near enough. Another one hundred and seventy pounds each later, on top of the annual insurance they already had, and they were hoping they had now covered everything. So much to remember and organise.

April 2015

Sunday the fifth – another car boot sale day. First one of the year, but they thought they would just try and raise some more funds. Not a bad day as they ended up with ninety pounds profit.

Wednesday the eighth – they bought the train tickets to the airport from London, another step nearer.

They also joined a slimming club – eek! It was probably a bit late to think about losing some weight, but every bit helps.

Wednesday the fifteenth – on the first weigh-in day, Tina lost one pound and Liz lost two and a half pounds. This was to be the only weigh-in they got to.

Sunday the nineteenth – this was another car boot day, with a profit of sixty pounds, and they also gave lots of their cards out and spread the word about what they were doing, which got quite a bit of interest.

Monday the twentieth – the Northern Echo, the Darlington and Stockton newspaper, got in touch and wanted to do a feature on them! The photographer was coming out the next day. Did they have enough time to pimp themselves though? They received the first copy of the Lady Biker magazine with their feature in and it was a double spread – fab!

Tuesday the twenty-first – they had the photoshoot, so they had to dust their bikes off and ride to a meeting point in Northallerton. It went really well, and the sun was shining for a change. It was their first photoshoot ever and was great fun. They also had a telephone interview, and they were told it would be in the paper tomorrow, things were moving fast now.

Thursday the twenty-third – another bit of excitement happened. They got a call from BBC Radio in York, inviting them to join them on Saturday for a live interview – this was scary and with no time to think about it, but they had to say yes. Liz was not sure if Tina could be trusted in a live situation as, most of the time, she could talk a glass eye to sleep.

Saturday the twenty-fifth – they had to get themselves up early and ready to set off to York. They got the train and managed to get a bit lost (getting lost was so much part of their normal day). Once they located it, they stood at the front door looking at the doorbell, with hesitation.

Tina suddenly announced, "Hang on a minute, I am not sure about going in here and feeling a bit nervous about this radio thing."

Liz replied, "Don't worry about it as there will only be us and the radio presenter and staff that will hear us."

Tina looked a bit shocked and replied, "What about the ten squillion people who will be listening to us?"

At that point Tina calmed down, but Liz went into a panic and turned to run.

She didn't get far, as Tina grabbed her arm.

"For fucks sake, we'll be fine. We have to do this," Tina said with her angry face, which can strike fear into the bravest of people.

So Liz meekly followed.

Right, deep breaths before Tina pressed the doorbell. They walked in sheepishly, still feeling a bit worried. They needn't to have felt nervous as they were made to feel very welcome and were taken into the Green Room, where they were plied with tea and coffee to calm them down.

Also in that room was Ian Burfield, who was being interviewed, too. He was really easy to chat to and made them feel more relaxed as, obviously, he was used to all this. So they spent the time explaining about the book and what they were doing, and he kept them calm, which was badly needed.

They could see the studio through the window in the

Green Room, which made them more nervous as it all looked a bit scary.

Then they were called into the studio, where they met Martin Barras, who was going to interview them. He immediately put them at ease and he explained that they were going to be in there for an hour and he would chat to them in between playing music. They were still a bit terrified though, as it was a first for them, probably the last, too!

He began with an introduction of who they were and explained what they were hoping to do. Then he asked who was going to go first and looked at Tina.

Who promptly said, "Well I think I will pass that one onto my friend, Liz, to explain."

She turned to look at Liz with a big grin on her face, knowing Liz would be mortified. As Tina was always the loud and gobby one, who has historically always been the first one to speak and always has plenty to say, this came as a bit of a shock to Liz, who scowled at her as she had to think on her feet (completely out of her comfort zone).

They managed to pull it off without incidents (Tina was kept under control somehow).

When they came out of there, they were shaking. They needed drink and food, this was so surreal, and they were on a high.

Once they got home, they listened to it on the playback. Well, they thought they sounded OK for novices. Maybe they would get another chance one day. The whole experience was amazing, and the studio and staff were brilliant.

Two weeks to go.

Thursday the thirtieth – the very important hair appointments needed to be slotted into their busy schedule, as they were needed to hide all the grey hairs that had been surfacing since they started this long journey.

Nine days to go.

May 2015

Friday the first – eight days to go. Has it really come round this quick?

Sunday the third – another shopping day for some last-minute stuff and they came back with flight socks and travel pillows (why?). Oh, also a Shewee each. Not sure who thought they needed one of these, but maybe they will be useful in the middle of the desert. It rained all day, so in and out of shops wasn't any fun. The thought of the sunshine kept them going.

Monday the fourth – they woke up to the sun shining. They thought they had better get used to this as they were heading to the sunshine state soon. Today was packing day. They needed to get all their things into two suitcases and one cabin case, this was going to be tricky. A few re-packs later and Liz was sorted. She then went to Tina's to supervise her and ensure she put everything in that she was supposed to from her list, as she couldn't be trusted not to forget something. Job done!

Friday the eighth – the last day at home today. They managed to get the urgent jobs done, such as getting their nails painted and eyebrows waxed. All very important stuff when you are going away.

One day to go.

Chapter 7
Day 1 Northallerton to London

Travelling from Northallerton to Gatwick Airport.

Today is the day they have been waiting months for, so, after a broken night's sleep due to excitement, it was an early start – not because they were leaving early, but because there was lots of prep to do.

Tina arrived at Liz's house around eleven a.m. This was very unusual for Tina to get anywhere on time, but probably the threat of being left behind motivated her as Liz was in charge of the tickets.

Last minute packing, followed by a trip into town to buy some breath freshener sprays (not sure why they needed these, but Tina thought they should have them). This was followed by a double check that they had passports, driving licences, credit cards, currency, and all the paperwork and maps required. It was at this point that Liz realised that Tina had forgotten her credit card (they would be unable to collect the hire car without it). She then had to ring Darran, who had to try and find one and bring it to the station when he came to see them off, although he appeared reluctant to find it for some reason... this became apparent when he met them at the station as he made Tina promise she wouldn't use it. Liz was sure he had some glue on it as it became very difficult to leave his hand and he started sweating at the prospect of handing it over.

They had three cases each, two large ones and a cabin

case, as well as a handbag, so they had to bungee the cabin cases onto the large ones and drag them along. Although Tina cheated, as a passing traveller at the station helped her get her cases into the station to Platform One at Northallerton Station.

Surprisingly, they had managed to get onto the platform about half an hour early. It must have been the first time Tina had been anywhere early, so it was nice to just sit down and wait for the train, whilst shivering in the chilly wind, dreaming of getting some sun and getting on those bikes.

The train arrived on time at 1.27p.m. It would take them directly to Kings Cross Station in London. They had booked seats in the First Class carriage, so they headed to the front of the train as it pulled in (there was a sign to say that First Class was going to be at the front). It was a bit fraught getting them and six cases onto the train, but they made it – they then realised that the first class carriage was at the back of the train, they had fallen at the first hurdle and this was just to be the start of the mishaps.

The train guard wouldn't let them get off the train, as there wasn't time, so they started dragging all the luggage through the carriages to get to the right one. They managed one carriage, then the conductor got cross and told them to wait and get off at Thirsk and walk down the platform to get to the right carriage. So they had to stand – so much for relaxing!

As the train was pulling to a stop, they readied themselves to get off quick and make a run down the platform to get to the carriage. The train door stuck but, after a few moments panicking, they got off, although one of Tina's cases almost dropped between the train and the platform down onto the lines, which caused another panicky moment!

They dragged the luggage to the back of the train and then

realised that they couldn't get onto their carriage as the train was too long for the small station. So they had to struggle onto the buffet carriage and work their way through that to their seats in the next carriage – by this stage they were so stressed they just had to order some wine with their lunch. This did help them unwind and chill out for the next couple of hours and get over the trauma of catching the train.

Liz ended up with a second bottle of wine and was wondering what she had let herself in for.

On arrival at Kings Cross they headed to check the train times that would take them from St Pancreas station to Gatwick Airport and they seemed to be running quite often. As they had open tickets they decided to wander over there at a nice, leisurely pace – until Tina spotted the shopping area, which is where things slowed down a bit.

The Mac shop caused the major issue, as Liz waited outside with the cases whilst Tina popped in for a quick look. After about ten minutes, Liz dragged all six cases into the shop (in a shift pattern) to find out where she had gone. She was spotted sitting at a mirror with one of the girls doing her make up – this was going to take some time, so Liz tried to look interested in the makeup racks to pass the time. But this didn't prove an easy task, so she had to resort to looking very bored in the hope Tina would get the hint – not her greatest plan as this didn't work well and impatience set in.

Eventually, they escaped out of that shop but still had to negotiate past a few more shops. Liz thought that there must be a way of getting Tina to walk past them without going in, so kept mentioning the train times and, if they hurried, they could catch the next one – all to no avail.

Sometime later, they managed to reach the first escalator

down. Tina decided to go first and balanced her cases onto the steps whilst hanging onto them for dear life. This didn't work as she couldn't keep hold of the heavier one and they all went tumbling down to the bottom. Closely followed by Tina, who was in a heap on the top of the cases. This caused great amusement for Liz, who was thinking this could be karma for making her go shopping and she was unable to help her due to her tearful laughter.

Luckily for Tina, there was a gentleman close behind them who proceeded to assist her in getting to her feet and picking her cases back up. The next problem was that there was a second escalator down to the platform, so Liz decided she would go first to avoid a re-run of the previous disaster. She raced ahead so that she wasn't going to be in the firing line of another mishap but, luckily, Tina had managed to get the hang of the steps with the help of the nice chap who had originally picked her up – literally.

They got themselves onto Platform A for the train to Gatwick, which was just pulling into the station. They had bought first class tickets, but the station guard said the train didn't have a first-class carriage – this was not what they were told when they purchased them from the local station, gutted.

At least they got on the right train and there was plenty of space, so it wasn't the disaster it could have been, and it was only about one hour to the airport. They passed the time by eating some chocolate Tina found in her bag, although it had melted a bit, but the taste was the same. Somehow, Liz managed to get it all over her jeans – not like her to waste any chocolate, so she was gutted for two reasons. Firstly, her jeans were dirty and, secondly, she had less chocolate to eat.

On arrival at the airport, they found a luggage trolley

which made their trip to the hotel next door a bit easier. When they got to their room, they had two double beds in it, much to Liz's relief!

They unpacked the clothes and toiletries they needed overnight, as they knew they had to get an early start the next morning. Whilst Tina was repacking her cases on the floor, she put her glasses down, then promptly stood back and squashed them. Luckily, they didn't break, they were just wonky – not a great start as she needed those to read.

They decided to go next door into the airport and find some food. There wasn't much there really, so they just had drinks and sandwiches, then had a scout around to find out where the check-in desk would be before heading back to get showered and have an early night.

Liz couldn't get the shower working, so Tina had to step up and use all her practical skills to kickstart it. Unfortunately, Tina was wearing her pyjamas whilst standing in the bath fixing the shower, so when the shower suddenly came on, she got a soaking – great, going on holiday with wet clothes in your case.

Chapter 8
Day 2 London to Las Vegas

London Gatwick to Las Vegas

They had set the alarm for seven a.m. Not that they got much sleep as they were too excited and Tina was doing her normal thing of getting up and down all night, making noises and putting lights on.

The usual morning rush around started and, as per usual, it took Tina ages to put her face on and run about picking all her stuff up with a bit of last-minute repacking. Then they had to try and bungee their cabin cases onto the top of one of the large cases, although this wasn't a very sturdy effort, and they soon wobbled off in the lift and on the walk to the airport. Eventually, they managed to find some luggage trolleys, so that was one problem sorted.

They had already sussed out where the check-in desk was so headed over to the queue, and, as they had booked Premium Economy seats, they had a designated check-in area, which was very efficient and speedy. So they soon got rid of the large cases and dashed off in search of food, as they were still without breakfast and coffees at this stage.

They made the decision to get through security first and, as they had booked into the airport lounge, they were looking forward to eating their way through that. They set off with just their cabin cases and handbags to get through security – this didn't take too long really, but, as usual, Liz was picked out of the queue for a search. They pulled her case to one side and ran an electronic scanner over it. Tina asked what they were doing, and he said he was looking for explosives – great!

Once they got away from security without any further incidents, they saw the signs for the Lounge and made a beeline as Liz was dreaming of food (again). Unfortunately for Liz, the path to the Lounge was littered with shops, which proved too much temptation for Tina and she had to stop at each one, with Liz following her, whinging about being hungry (her pleas for food were totally ignored by Tina).

Tina had picked up some perfume she wanted, and whilst she set off for the queue to pay for it, Liz wandered around browsing in the shop, as she fully expected to see Tina emerge from the checkout at any minute. But oh no – when Liz got fed up of waiting and went to search for Tina, she found her in the makeup section getting her face done (again). She hadn't even got as far as the pay desks!

Liz thought that enough was enough and announced she was going to the Lounge without her and duly set off to locate it. In the Lounge, she got tea and breakfast and managed to chill out and read for a bit, whilst watching the planes taxiing on the runway. Eventually, Tina turned up after getting lost without her navigator by her side and just had time to get a coffee and order some breakfast before the gate was announced.

Off they went again, dragging along their cabin cases through the maze of corridors to find the gate. A lot of the walkways were moving ones, so Liz went on those whilst Tina decided it would be quicker to just walk. Therefore a race developed; to find out which was actually the quickest and who could get to the end of the corridor first. It turns out that the moving walkways were quicker, so a winner emerged on the race to Gate 32. The last lot of exercise they were going to get for a while.

After a short wait they started to board. They had priority boarding, so they could get on and get settled before everyone else boarded – good idea with Tina around.

There was a blanket and a pillow waiting for them, so Tina got the window seat and was under strict instructions not to get up and down all through the flight. Liz wanted to settle down and try and sleep a bit – obviously, this request fell on deaf ears and Tina couldn't sit still.

The flight was fairly uneventful. They got regular visits from the trolleys bringing them food and drinks, the gin and tonics were very welcome. Ten and a half hours later, they landed in Las Vegas. The time was one-fifty p.m. but the UK time was nine-fifty p.m. (eight hours difference), so they got a bit disorientated with that.

Towards the end of the flight Tina wanted to get washed and changed before landing but of course her clothes were in the case that was held in the overhead luggage compartment. So, ignoring the pleas from Liz about not disturbing her, Tina squeezed past her to get into the aisle, then proceeded to open the overhead locker with difficulty. Because they were first on the plane, their bags were at the back of the locker. So Tina had to move the other bags out of the way to get to her bag, which of course caused everyone else's bags to fall out into the aisle. Due to her height issues, this caused havoc and a few other travellers had to get disturbed from their seats to help her and also to rescue their bags and put them all back in. Through all this commotion, Liz stayed hiding behind her sleep mask and pretended to be asleep.

Eventually, Tina got her hands on her bag and headed off to the toilets. When she got there, the toilet was vacant but, when she walked in she was hit with a horrendous aroma. So she held her breath as much as possible and got her quick change and wash; then rushed out, straight into another passenger who was waiting to use the toilet. The aroma followed her out of the door and the waiting passenger just stared at her, obviously thinking she had a problem. Tina quickly pointed out that she was innocent of the crime and ran back to her seat, squeezing past Liz again.

They got off the plane and followed everyone else to get through customs. Tina went first and waited at the other side whilst Liz got through. In the meantime, Tina was told off for loitering near the customs area and moved on, so she had to hide round the corner to wait for Liz.

When they emerged from the Arrivals area, there was a chauffeur waiting for them with their names on a board. They got his attention and were led to the car, which turned out to be a black limousine with leather seats and blue strip-lights inside.

Tina talked to the driver all the way to the hotel, so they were lucky he took them straight there and didn't dump them somewhere. On the way to the hotel they noticed that he had left his boot open so they got a bit worried thinking about their cases and underwear getting spread all over the road behind them but fortunately everything was in one piece and arrived safe and sound along with them, the driver couldn't get away quick enough as he clearly had sore ears and was probably terrified.

It only took around an hour from landing to arriving at the hotel so they were very impressed with the efficiency, although, in reality, it probably had more to do with the fact that no one wanted to spend much time near them.

They checked into their hotel, which was amazing, and they couldn't believe the amount of gaming tables they had to go through to get to the lift for the room. The room was quite large and had two double beds – yippee! Tina decided she was going to go out and investigate, whilst Liz opted for a couple of hours sleep before her friend arrived from London – did we mention we had a third occupant for four nights?

After a nice nap, Liz was awoken by Tina crashing back into the room. This was lucky, otherwise she would have stayed there for the night. They managed to get showers and unpack and by this time they got a text to say that Jackie was on her way to the hotel in a taxi. So they headed down to reception to meet her. After they had smuggled her into their room (this was a necessary move due to the excessive amounts of money the hotel wanted just for her to sleep in the room), she got showered, then they dashed off to hit the town.

By this time it was dark, so the city was lit up and was an amazing sight for three Vegas virgins.

They wandered around with their city map, trying not to look like tourists – this didn't work well!

There were lots of homeless people on the streets, all with unusual stories handwritten onto cardboard signs about their circumstances. Of course, Tina had to stop to talk to each one and give them lessons in life and lecture them about living on the streets. Liz and Jackie wandered slightly ahead, hoping no one would connect them to Tina – oh, the embarrassment!

They managed to get Tina going by promising food, so they set off looking for sustenance and found some sort of steak house place (although Liz is a vegetarian). Luckily, they had a veggie option on the menu, which was duly ordered and tasted disgusting. So, after a complaint to the waitress, they managed to get a refund for that meal. The drinks were good though!

By this time the jet lag was starting to set in, so they headed back to their hotel through a maze of slot machines and gambling tables. Oh dear, someone forgot to set the string trail. Navigating the way to the room was complicated, to say the least, but they were so grateful to see a bed at this stage, they just crashed out. As there were only two beds, Jackie and Liz had to share. Liz being under threat of death for snoring – who cares ha-ha.

Stayed at the Bellagio hotel, Las Vegas Strip.

Chapter 9
Day 3 Las Vegas

Today is Monday and the first full day of Vegas, yahoo!

After a good crashed-out sleep, they managed to find a nice café within the hotel; after a lot of getting lost and going round in circles, all of which ended up at the gaming tables. They got themselves into an orderly queue (as the British are good at). Once the menu had arrived it was a case of filling their faces with everything they possibly could in anticipation of a busy day ahead, and hoping they didn't need to buy lunch, so could save a few dollars there.

With full bellies, they set off to find the pool, which took some navigating. After being stopped a couple of times by the pool guards, they managed to get sunbeds and get themselves settled for a busy day of sunbathing and relaxing. They obviously didn't look like the normal clientele.

The pool area was fantastic, so they stripped off to their bikinis and basked in the sunshine, with the occasional ordering of frozen cocktails from one of the many passing waitresses. Little did they realise at that time, but absolutely everyone they spoke to wanted a tip (they hadn't budgeted for this cost, so, after a few days of giving their hard-earned spending money away, they decided they had to be more careful and just give token tips).

By mid-afternoon, they all headed off back to the room – which was quite a hike, actually – where they all got showered and changed, then another hike to get out of the hotel to hit the town. Everything was so big.

At this point, food was at the forefront of their mind. After managing all day on a big breakfast and frozen cocktails, the hunger pangs were setting in. All they could think of was food, so that was the first task of the night and they found a nice place in the Mile Long Shopping Mall! Yes, it really is a mile long and you can get totally lost, as they did many times. The roof of the mall is a blue sky with a few clouds, giving you the illusion that it is daytime all the time, very unsettling!

After a good feed, it was time to have a look around the shops for some souvenirs and they found just the thing – steam irons! Duly purchasing one each, no one was going to believe that the irons were their souvenirs from Vegas. Feeling completely nutty, they tried to hide them in the bags as they didn't want anyone to see what they had bought. It was just so ridiculous – who goes to Vegas and buys an iron!

Next stop was an oxygen bar. Nothing could stop Jackie and Tina testing the oxygen and floating tanks. Liz decided to keep her money for something more interesting and left them to it so she could have a wander around in peace. Although you couldn't go far as, once you got lost round there you would be missing forever.

After an exhausting day (or was it night, one is never really sure once you get lost in the mall), they faced another trek back to the hotel room for a very early start tomorrow. They managed to get to bed by about two a.m. – result!

They managed to get through the first day without any major issues but there were plenty more opportunities to go yet.

Chapter 10
Day 4 Las Vegas (Grand Canyon)

The alarms went off around three-thirty a.m. for the trip to the Grand Canyon. At the time of booking, it made sense to get the morning trip, although neither could remember why this was. It didn't seem such a good plan now.

After struggling to get up and dressed, all still half asleep (or maybe just still asleep, but who cares as there was fun to be had today). First stop was the café for breakfast. Yes, it really was open for breakfast at four a.m., although it was the first time any of them had experienced this time of day, unless it involved heading for bed.

After being told to wait outside for the pick-up at five a.m., they waited and waited, but it seemed a bit strange that there were no signs of anything happening. After questioning this, it appeared they had got it wrong and had been waiting in the wrong place – no surprise there then. Luckily, someone on the door directed them to the back of the hotel where there was a coach park and pick up area, which they knew nothing about. A mad run to get there ensued before the coach arrived, not an easy feat whilst still half asleep.

A minibus arrived just after they found the meeting point. After a bit of panicking, they just got on it. Luckily, it took a bit of time to get to the airfield, so this gave a bit of a tour through the city as it had others to collect on the way.

At the airfield there was a check-in procedure to go

through. Apparently this was the case even for small planes and short trips, the worst possible part of this was the dreaded weigh in – oh no, this couldn't be happening, were they all going to get on the same plane?

Thank goodness they didn't make any comments and managed to just scrape through this most embarrassing of situations. They were then shuffled through to a waiting area to stay there and wait for the pilot, who arrived shortly after to select the people he was taking on his small plane and to give the safety briefing.

They were then escorted outside towards a fixed-wing plane with a small number of other people. The sight of the plane struck immediate fear into Liz, who not only had a fear of flying but also of heights. There were approximately twelve seats on this plane and Liz and Tina were instructed to sit at the very rear of the plane, in single seats, on opposite sides (had this guy had been forewarned...). It appeared he took a fancy to Jackie and selected her to be his co-pilot and sit up front at the controls with him, which she was well up for, and off they went; rattling down the runway.

Forty minutes of fear for Liz, who kept her eyes closed the whole way there and missed the Hoover Dam and the amazing scenery. Tina was going to film it on the GoPro, so this kept her quiet on the whole journey; no mean feat!

After landing on a small airfield, they went through the small airport to wait for a shuttle bus that would take them to the two locations best suited to see the canyon. First stop was the Skywalk.

After getting off the bus there was plenty of time to wander around in a daze at the Canyon. It was an amazing sight, so lots of photos were taken along with some film (although they all looked the same in the end). Then came the really scary moment of getting onto the Skywalk. They were provided with covers to put on over their shoes and were told to leave bags and cameras in a locker, so they were unable to take anything on with them – gutted!

The whole point of going somewhere like this was to capture the whole experience on film, but cameras, bags, etc. are not allowed to be taken on. It soon dawned on them the reason why – they had their own photographer who wanted to sell their pictures.

There were some that managed to sneak their cameras on, so they were told very sharpish by Tina to go back. She informed the staff, too, so they were not happy. Totally unfair when some can do it and others can't, though!

Looking a mile down through a glass floor was quite surreal and captivating. The professional photographer was waiting on the walkway to take photos of all the tourists and to sell them later, although it was fun doing different poses as if they were hanging off the side and sitting on the glass path – definitely worth it though.

As lunch was included in the trip, they set off to get fed and sat outside to eat the BBQ meal. This didn't include much for vegetarians though. There were quite a few paths around to follow for different views, so they all wandered off a bit on their own, enjoying some alone time, which was to prove almost impossible on this trip. Tina had wandered off a bit further, so Liz and Jackie eventually found her and managed to catch her red-handed trying to leave her name on a wooden shack – really should get some reins for this girl.

The half day trip was almost over, so time to catch the shuttle bus back to the airfield, and for the ride home. They did get a great photo of them all with the pilot by the plane before leaving, too. Worryingly, the plane was tied down and the wind was so strong it was a struggle just to stand up – oh dear, the trip back wouldn't be fun.

That was a severe understatement! After taking the same seats on the way back, the plane set off down the runway for take-off, which was terrifying on its own, but the journey back proved to be horrific. The plane was thrown around so severely that they had to keep their seat belts on the whole time. The forty-minute trip back took an hour – never again!

Back at the hotel, after some stiff drinks were had, they managed to get themselves showered and changed and headed out foraging for food again. Liz was still shaking after the plane trip back, the drinks hadn't helped much, so maybe more were needed.

The first stop to make was in the mall at the iron shop. Tina had tried to use her iron, only to fail miserably, then Liz and Jackie had to try theirs and discovered they weren't working like they were shown in the demonstration. That meant creased clothes again then. All three irons were taken back to the shopkeeper and, after a very long-winded explanation from Tina, with some back-up from the other two about how disgusted they were that they had been conned and that they didn't work, etc. etc. the man in the shop took them all off them and proceeded to show them how to use the irons properly. It appeared that Tina had been incorrectly operating hers, along with the other two as well (they need salt, apparently, although where do you buy salt in Vegas?). The worst thing was that the person showing how to use them correctly was a man (so much for women being equal, three girls couldn't even use an iron without instruction from a man, useless!).

Totally embarrassed and very red-faced, they had to admit defeat and left, holding their irons – a drink was needed and fast.

Next stop was the Venetian Hotel. So many people had recommended a visit to this place that it was always on the list to do. It was enormous (just like everything in Vegas). Canals were running through the hotel, with gondolas ready to take you on a ride through the hotel if you wanted – so weird!

If the price had been better, they decided it would have been fun, but the funds could be better directed elsewhere. So they declined and continued walking around mini Venice and found an Italian restaurant (of which there were many in this hotel, for some reason). Lots of yummy food and drink and a big bill – mostly for the tips, they expected, which was cut drastically by Jackie, who was on a mission to get value for money! During the meal a photographer came round and was taking everyone's photographs for free. Wow, something for free? In Vegas, too? It turned out that she took your photo for free but sold you the actual photo – another con for the English tourists!

With full bellies and feeling considerably lighter, financially, they continued wandering around the hotel and found the slot machines, not that they were easily missed anywhere in Vegas.

Apparently, free drinks are on offer in the hotels if you are playing on the machines. This sounded like a good plan, so a gambling machine was picked and then they ordered three drinks through the machine. All they needed to do was wait for them. In the meantime, Jackie had some loose change so decided she would have a gamble as, by this point, none of them had gambled anything and it seemed rude not to have a go whilst in Vegas. Into the slot went her change, then nothing happened.

"Strange," she thought.

Then she couldn't get a refund out, therefore couldn't have a gamble. The coin was only stuck! A passing gambler mentioned that you can't use small change on the machines, it jams them up. Well, of course this was not something any of them were aware of, so she pressed the button for the maintenance man and, in a moment of panic, all three ran away from that machine and perched themselves at another one in sight of the jammed one.

Just in the nick of time, as it happened, as the girl with the tray of drinks appeared at the old machine and couldn't understand why no one was there. So, trying to look innocent, they put their heads down and tried to look interested in the machine they had chosen, feeling very embarrassed as she then went away again, taking all the drinks with her – arghhhh, nooooo, not the drinks!

After a few more moments had elapsed, a maintenance engineer turned up at the machine and proceeded to fix it. This was quick service, but they must have been worried they were missing out on some gamblers. By now they were starting to feel very guilty, so clubbed together and put in about five dollars each to have a go at the slot machine. After all, you can't visit Vegas without at least one gamble (on a working machine anyway). To cut a long story short, it was all lost – what a surprise! Well that was it, the whole gambling budget blown. They got out of the hotel as quick as possible.

It had been such a long day, and it was almost morning again, so off to their beds they went; after being up about twenty-two hours by this time.

Chapter 11
Day 5 Las Vegas

After a good sleep, well apart from the snoring interruptions by Tina, their stomachs forced them out of bed and off to breakfast – that's if they could find the café again.

Another good feed and off to the pool they went. This was their last full day in this hotel, so it was the last chance to catch a bit of sunbathing and chilling out with their books or music on the sunbeds being served frozen cocktails.

Daytime was fairly uneventful, as they had a lazy day and some naps to rejuvenate them for the night ahead, which involved miles of walking. This is normal here as the only way to see everything.

They decided they would turn right out of the hotel, as they had been left to the Venetian and across the road to the Mile Mall but not to the right side, where there were many famous hotels to be visited.

The first stop was to the Harley shop and café, where they bought some t-shirts – loads cheaper than at home, too. Happy with their bargains, they passed so many shops to trawl through and eventually settled on one that they thought was worth investigating further. In this shop Jackie tried most of the jeans on and eventually settled for a gorgeous sparkly pair with a sparkly belt and Tina got some t-shirts, so they were all happy as they all had something to take home with them.

They continued on and found a roadhouse, where they

ordered food. Unfortunately, the vegetarian option of a wrap was so disgusting it had to go back. Never mind, at least there were plenty of puds!

Right, hotel tour next!

The first one was New York, New York. They were amazed that anyone can wander in and out of the hotels and just look around, although they all look pretty similar – full of slot machines! This hotel happened to have a roller coaster, so Jackie and Tina decided to go on it. As there was only two seats, Liz offered to look after the bags instead – good move!

They managed to keep hold of their dinner though.

They then went into the Luxor, which had some exhibitions on, but, unfortunately, they were closed that evening – just their luck.

The next hotel they wanted to visit was the Monterey Bay, which apparently had some sharks in a pool there – this area was closed, too. It was like wandering round ghost hotels and it almost felt like they were the only ones there.

They then went into Excalibur. It was like a fantasy land. They ordered some drinks and stayed at the bar, passing the time whilst Tina talked at the poor bar man.

It was such a long walk back to their hotel, it seemed like miles and miles. Everything was so big and so far away, or so it seemed.

Chapter 12
Day 6 Las Vegas

Another sunny day in this amazing city, although it was the last in this hotel and check-out loomed.

After the long walk to and from breakfast, the packing began.

Three girls running around a hotel room trying to locate all their possessions with a deadline was chaotic.

"Anyone seen my phone charger?"

Someone packed it thinking it was theirs, etc. etc.

Well, after the successful smuggling of Jackie into the hotel room, there was just one last gauntlet to run – to the checkout desks. She sauntered to the waiting area in reception, trying to look innocent (not easy) and Liz and Tina went off to pick a desk to check out at. Although it was rather like an airport terminal, with the number of desks all lined up.

The lady who was doing the checking-out asked a simple question.

"Have you enjoyed your stay with us?"

Bad move.

Tina promptly said that it was the worst hotel they had ever stayed in and that the stay was terrible. The receptionist was horrified and picked up her phone to call the manager, but Liz had to stop her mid-flow and explain that it was Tina's idea of a joke. It wasn't appreciated though! So much for the Anglo-American alliance, Tina just ruined it.

As the check-in time at the next hotel wasn't until four p.m., all the luggage was dumped into the hotel luggage room, so that gave more time and freedom for... shopping!

The Mile Mall was fast becoming a torture walk for those who didn't enjoy shopping. Well actually this only applied to Liz. The shopping escape looked promising when the Hard Rock Café was spotted. This surely was going to be a must visit place. This was a big let-down. Not only was it a long queue to get in, but the service was also poor, and it only had snacks available, which were very expensive. Time to move on and find another café that served real food,

After more shopping and eating, it was almost time to check in at the next hotel (Planet Hollywood), where Liz and Tina would meet their tour leader from Eagle Riders and the rest of the group.

Back to the Bellagio to collect all the cases. The attempt to cross the road (the next hotel was opposite) with three cases each for Liz and Tina and one large one for Jackie was terrifying. There were a few attempts at making it across, for those of you who have ever tried to cross the road in Vegas will know how difficult it is without luggage, never mind laden down with seven cases.

After regrouping and all surviving the road-crossing feat, they looked for the entrance to Planet Hollywood. This was easier said than done! The only way in seemed to be to go back into the Mile Mall to find the entrance, where they discovered a café. In need of food and fuel, they plonked themselves in there to get the feeling back in their hands and feet – phew, this was lovely.

The arrangement was to meet the tour guide at four p.m., so they rushed off to find the reception, which was well hidden by more slot machines, and got checked in. Another long hike to find the room through the maze of corridors, which turned out to be very pokey and a complete contrast to the luxury in the Bellagio.

Yet again, Jackie was smuggled in as she was heading back to the UK in a couple of hours but needed somewhere to shower, etc. first.

After saying their goodbyes (Liz and Tina would not be back by the time Jackie's taxi arrived), they set off to find the reception lobby and the tour guide. They only had half an hour to find their rooms, get their bike gear on, and get back to the lobby for the arranged meeting.

Feeling very excited, but very nervous, little did they know at the time what they had let themselves in for. Looking back, neither of them are sure they would actually do it again, but maybe in a few years' time when it's been forgotten.

The tour guide, Don, was lurking in the lobby and had already managed to find some of the group and get them together. In total, there were nineteen people. Fourteen bikers and the rest were pillion, but Liz and Tina were the only lady riders.

The downstairs lobby was the meeting area and had doors opening up into a parking and drive-through area. This was where there were a couple of minibuses ready to ferry the group to the Harley Davidson shop in Vegas. Everyone scrambled onto the buses that were going to take them to collect their bikes, which would be their constant companions for the next ten days.

It only took about fifteen minutes to arrive at the shop, where Tina spotted a long line of bikes all ready to be taken delivery of. Hoping that they had got the bikes they asked for, they hopped off the bus and headed into the shop to the rental counter.

It was time to register and complete the paperwork before they could be introduced to their bikes. After signing all the endless forms, etc. they were asked for credit cards – they looked at each other with horror as they hadn't brought them in the rush to get there. It was explained that without a valid credit card (debit card wouldn't do) they would not be allowed to take the bikes away. After the initial panic, Liz remembered that they had left them in their room and that hopefully Jackie would still be there. So a quick phone call established she was, and, with some direction, she managed to find both of the cards and give the card numbers over the phone, which they were satisfied with (Darran would be horrified – Tina had used the card!).

It soon became apparent that this reception area was disorganised chaos. They had never been told they needed a credit card, so they were lucky they had taken them. The staff then tried to get everyone to sign to say that they would all pay for fuelling the bikes – this had all been prepaid and, luckily, the email confirmations and invoices were on emails stored on Liz's phone. Others in the group got quite irate about this as some of them had just got off a flight and were tired before they got there, so tempers were starting to fray – not problems already!

Eventually, after a couple of hours, they let everyone take the bikes. After a quick tour round the bike (very quick as everyone else had ridden Harleys before) the whole group very carefully set off and followed Don back to the hotel and its car park area under the hotel. This ride was very tricky, to say the least, as not only were they riding strange bikes but they were also riding on the wrong side of the road, trying to watch where Don was going and trying to keep up to make sure neither got stuck at lights, etc. Very stressful; and they were hoping this wasn't a sign of things to come – how wrong they were!

Meanwhile, after parking the bikes in a specific line, which they were not much good at and raised a few tuts, Don started dishing out kit, etc. This included an Eagle Rider jacket, a leather-bound folder with maps in it, and a new GoPro camera each – impressed!

Of course the jacket that Tina ordered was too small (well it would have to be Tina's that was wrong) due to her increased bust (not sure what happened there), but there were a few different sizes so she eventually found one to fit her correctly.

At that point Don gave everyone fifteen minutes to take all the kit back to their rooms and get changed for dinner – this was the start of stressful rushing around and Don obviously started as he meant to go on!

Running back to their room, when it was found through the maze of hotel corridors, Jackie had left for home so there was just time to quickly change and run back again. Although, Tina wanted to put her face on – no time for this (Tina has no concept of time). They were almost late back, but Liz insisted that they were not late anywhere!

The first night's meal was included in the trip so that everyone could bond with their fellow riders. There were three couples from the UK and the rest of the group were all from other countries, including Italy, Sweden, Argentina, France, etc. with different levels of spoken English. So communicating wasn't that easy. Although everyone was tired already, at least a good feed was had and then, one by one, they all headed back to their rooms. It was quite late really, as they were told they had to meet for breakfast at seven a.m. so they could be away by eight a.m., due to the long day they faced tomorrow. Apparently, they all had to go back to the Harley shop as one of the bikes had broken down then there was three hundred and fifteen miles to ride before sleep.

They just looked at each other in horror. Is this what they signed up for? Where was the gentle morning starts, and the sightseeing stops, and the chilling out they had seen on the internet adverts and the brochures? For those that watched the same videos and read the same literature, IT DOES NOT EXIST.

Stayed at the Planet Hollywood Resort, Las Vegas Strip, for one night

Chapter 13
Day 7 - Las Vegas to Bakersfield

LAS VEGAS TO MAMMOTH LAKES, THREE HUNDRED
AND FIFTEEN MILES PLUS LOTS OF EXTRA MILES TO
BAKERSFIELD

The alarm was set for six a.m. Oh god, they were feeling so tired, and it was only the first day on the bikes. Liz had to drag Tina out of bed and off to breakfast by seven a.m. They wandered round for what seemed like ages; around all the slot machines and up and down escalators, looking for the breakfast area – fed up already!

They found the food area and stuffed their faces (normal for them), then had to retrace their steps to get back to their room and pack (again). As they had three cases each, and all their bike kit, this was no mean feat. Then Tina wouldn't leave the room until she had put her face on, with Liz stood behind her trying to hurry her up.

"We need to go right NOW, Tina!"

This same statement was said every morning with endless repetitiveness. She had no concept of time and Liz didn't realise how apparent this was going to be on a daily basis.

Struggling with their luggage, and with Tina's face done, they set off to the meeting point in the car park where they found everyone else already there – oops. Liz decided that wasn't going to happen again. They had a tough girlie reputation to hold up on behalf of all the girl bikers out there.

There was a minibus that took all the cases and they were allowed to keep a rucksack each, which was fastened to the rear of the bikes with the bungee ropes they had taken with them (very organised!). So, all kitted up and bikes started, the sound was amazing with all the Harley's ticking over. They still had that excited feeling (although this soon faded). Don announced that they all had to call in at the Harley shop on the way to collect one of the bikes that had broken down the previous day. So off they went in convoy, in the same direction they had taken the previous evening to collect them.

Of course, when they all pulled up at the shop the bike wasn't ready, so everyone ended up waiting around for a couple of hours before they could set off. Which wasn't too bad as it gave everyone a chance to chat to the other members of the group, drink tea, and take advantage of a rare toilet being available.

Eventually, they were all rounded up and herded together with some basic instructions about the next move, which was to be to Death Valley, where they would stop for a break and some photos. In Vegas the weather was great, but it became very chilly on the next stage of the route and they were both shivering by the time they got to Death Valley.

They got time to wander off and stretch their legs and, after lots of photos were taken, everyone got ready to set off again. Apparently lots of people had fainted due to the heat on previous tours. Really? They all asked. They had four layers on, and this was supposed to be one of the hottest places on earth. They might have known that the English weather was going to follow them.

Two months later, in Death Valley, the recorded temperature was thirty-two degrees and the lowest for that year was eighteen degrees, apparently. They were sure it was more like ten degrees – brrrrr.

After an hour of riding away from Death Valley, Don pulled everyone to a stop as it had started to rain, so they could all put on wet weather gear. There was a sort of toilet in this car park area, which was actually a shed with a hole in the ground – horrifying, but, when you have to go, you have to go, just wish those Shewee's had been handy.

It seemed to rain for ages. It also rained in Tina's helmet the whole journey, which, when added to the tears she was shedding, made her look a mess when they stopped.

Next stop was for a late lunch at a ranch café. Thank goodness for some food and tea! There was a major problem for Liz, as she was a tea drinker and it seemed most of the cafes only sold coffee. Luckily she had brought a stash of tea bags and kept them in her bum bag, which was worn at all times, so she could just ask for hot water; although she got some funny looks. Well, who asks for hot water in a cafe!

They were soon rounded up again by Don. This rushing about soon became the norm on this trip and sometimes they didn't even get time to eat as they were on constant deadlines – just whose bright idea was this trip?

The next leg of the journey was one of the worst they had ever experienced. It poured down, so everyone got all cold and wet and to top that the cross winds were horrific; everyone struggled to keep the bikes upright. This was a nightmare and such hard work, too.

Everyone stopped at a garage after a couple of hours and managed to get some chocolate and drinks to keep them going. They were all exhausted as it was about seven p.m. by this time and they were so far behind schedule.

Don got everyone together and announced that although the tour was supposed to take them to Mammoth Lakes, the roads had been closed due to excessive snowfalls – this was May, wasn't it? Due to this problem they were going to be diverted, which involved further riding on this, the longest day ever, to a town called Bakersfield. They were tired, cold, and wet, so this news just destroyed everyone, but they had no choice but to keep going.

They all set off again, through severe winds and rain; then eventually through darkness, following Don to a hotel in Bakersfield. Unfortunately there were quite a few lanes and roads on the way, and because it was dark and the town lights were so poor they struggled to see in front of them. Some of the group got a bit disorientated but eventually everyone all made it to the hotel car park and couldn't get off the bikes quick enough.

By this time it was around nine p.m.; everyone was handed their room keys and they went off to find their rooms. Tina was in tears (again) so ran into the room and locked herself in the bathroom and ran the bath. It looked like it was down to Liz to get six cases in then! This was no easy task, and she was on the verge of tears and cold, too. Unfortunately she couldn't get into the bathroom for about an hour, as Tina had decided to have a soak; leaving Liz needing the toilet and a shower and there was nowhere for her to go – wonder how much liquid the cups could hold, hmm, maybe not a good idea to pee in the hotel cups.

After being allowed into the bathroom and with both of them now cleaned up and having had a chance to wind down a bit, it was too late to get food. Tina managed to persuade the kitchen staff to bring tea and toast to the room. This was their evening meal – they felt like they couldn't go on at this point and it had to be the lowest point in the trip.

The good news was that they got a double bed each and these were so appealing they just crashed out. By this time it was about eleven p.m. and a week's sleep would have been welcome. Unfortunately, there was only a few hours before they had to be up, and it all started all over again.

They stayed at the Holiday Inn, Bakersfield, for one night.

Chapter 14
Day 8 -Bakersfield to Yosemite

MAMMOTH LAKES TO YOSEMITE, ONE HUNDRED AND FIFTY MILES (STARTED FROM BAKERSFIELD, SO EVEN MORE MILES)

Another early start, as the alarm now knows to go off at six a.m. every morning. It was the normal routine of dragging Tina out of bed and heading for breakfast, then Tina's cement to put on before she can leave the room, and the normal dragging of all the cases to the minibus – this was to become a normal way of life for the days ahead. They could not see the light at the end of the tunnel and this was only their second day on the bikes. At this stage they weren't sure they could make it to the end, but the fact that they knew they couldn't fail had something to do with their determination to make it.

The weather had improved a bit by today and, luckily, there wasn't any more rain on the trip, or the severe winds they had experienced yesterday. They were still exhausted, but they just had to follow the leader and keep up all the way to Sierra City, where everyone stopped for lunch.

This was a small town and only had a couple of cafes, so Liz, Tina, and another two of the bikers decided to walk a bit further along to avoid the long queue, as all the group went into the nearest café. Tina found what looked like a lovely spot, so they took a table outside and placed their orders. They waited, and waited, and waited, had they been forgotten? The clock was ticking and by now they knew what a hard taskmaster the leader was, so they knew they didn't have much time.

Eventually, all the food arrived after what seemed like a long, long time! Just as they were tucking in, one of the group came looking for them and rounded all four of them up. They had to ask for the food to be wrapped up so they could eat it at the next stop, even if it was cold. Off they set again, rush, rush, rushing everywhere.

On the route to the hotel by the entrance to Yosemite Park, Liz and Tina got left behind as some traffic lights changed on a bridge. They sat there for at least ten minutes, waiting for them to turn to green. They had no idea that this was quite normal, but in the end Tina took the decision to just go through them anyway, so Liz followed. Otherwise they were going to be so far behind, and there was no traffic in the opposite direction – well, they hoped not!

After getting a bit lost, they found the hotel and got checked in. Don had organised a trip into Yosemite, and he had entrance tickets for everyone. They all followed him into the park and found somewhere to leave the bikes so they could have a walk about and take in some views.

They walked to an amazing waterfall and took in the atmosphere of this beautiful park. There was going to be another group going deeper into the park, but a small group, including Liz and Tina, decided they were going to find their own way back to the hotel – what a stupid decision.

This was just a small park, wasn't it? They all rode round and round and couldn't find their way out of the park. Tired and hungry, they were completely fed up (again) when, by a complete fluke, they spotted the exit! There were no exit signs, or anything that resembled the way out, and lots of the roads were on a one-way system, so they had just been riding round and round for what seemed like hours.

At least there was a nice room at the hotel that had a balcony and chairs that looked onto a stream and a forest area, along with a bit of wildlife, too. Shame it wasn't warm enough to sit outside though, the weather was still not being kind.

Their leader decided that he would organise a get-together in his room. Maybe he had noticed everyone was getting tired and fed up! Liz and Tina decided to call in as he offered pizzas (yummy). When they got in, he only had meat pizzas and as Liz was a vegetarian they had to go and find food somewhere else, which was limited to one bar at the hotel. By this time they were feeling very tired, unsociable, and hungry.

They went across to the bar and managed to order a small snack, as they didn't have much on offer to eat; then they headed to their beds, and it was only nine p.m. Who said this was fun?

Stayed at the Yosemite View Lodge for one night

Chapter 15
Day 9 Yosemite to San Francisco

YOSEMITE TO SAN FRANCISCO, TWO HUNDRED
MILES

Today they got up with a bit more enthusiasm after a good
night's sleep and the prospect of getting into San Francisco,
which was the highlight of the trip for them. So, at last, they
had something to look forward to and a break for their bums.

After another early start and breakfast, they were on the
road again. This living out of suitcases isn't as good as it
sounds.

They seemed to ride on and on at a fast pace, but mostly
on a lot of freeways. So much for strict speed limits, as no one
seemed to be sticking to them. If you did the correct speed you
got left behind and no one waited for you either, as they found
out a few times. It was a case of keep up with the pack or get
lost, which was extremely easy to do.

On one of the freeways the pace had slowed down, due to
a large fire in a field next to the road which was being attended
to by firemen (this attracted their attention but no time to look
though). They had to ride through thick smoke. This would
never happen at home! It was quite scary, actually, as they
weren't sure where the front riders were. It was like riding
through fog.

At the next fuel stop they were all given instructions for
the route into San Francisco. They were all to stick close

together at any cost due to the heavy traffic and lane crossing as they went in over the bridge. What an amazing sight in front of them, they couldn't wait. At last they could spend two nights in the same place, and sleep!

The hotel wasn't far and was situated on Fisherman's Wharf, so close to the pier and all the restaurants and shops. The parking area was quite big and all the bikes had to be linked together and locked up before they could get checked into the hotel. Although, this was now a nightly routine. They were so thrilled that they had a full day off the next day, and the night visit to Alcatraz, too. This was going to be fun.

They couldn't wait to get showered, changed, and get out there. They had a wander around and eventually settled on a restaurant, where they filled their faces without having to rush about – bliss.

All the shops were open late, too. Tina found one that sold remote control devices that they could sync with their GoPro cameras. This would be much easier to start and stop filming if they were strapped onto the handlebars of the bikes. Tina bargained with the shop man and managed to get them for one hundred dollars each (although they found out later that they can be bought at home for thirty pounds).

At the time they were happy with their bargain. As they tried to pay for them, Tina's purse zip got stuck and she couldn't get her money out. Damn, did Darran have a remote control for her purse at home? He must have just known she was going to buy something! After much force, she got it open and duly paid for their new toys. They headed off to bed, looking forward to a bit of a sleep-in tomorrow.

They stayed at the Radisson Fisherman's Wharf hotel for two nights.

Chapter 16
Day 10 San Francisco

SAN FRANCISCO - FULL DAY

Today they woke up with much excitement and trepidation as this day was going to be one the highlights of the trip – they had an evening trip to Alcatraz lined up. It was going to be so spooky, being on the island at night, they couldn't wait. Also, they had all day to amuse themselves as they didn't have to be at the meeting point until around three p.m.

For some reason it was much easier to get out of bed today. Maybe because they had a bit of a lay-in and they knew that they didn't have to rush anywhere – the relief was overwhelming.

Their next thought turned to breakfast. As the hotel didn't actually serve breakfast, everyone was given vouchers for a diner around the corner so they could have a limited breakfast in there, but any extras had to be paid for.

As they got sat down after standing in a long queue, they asked what they were entitled to with the vouchers. The waitress explained what was available and Tina, as usual, didn't listen properly and ordered toast, too (which wasn't on the list). After the waitress took the order (she sighed a lot as she did this – obviously not happy in her job), it was pointed out to Tina that she would have to pay for the toast, which was met with a look of horror on her face as she hadn't brought her purse with her. This was pretty normal behaviour for Tina as she rarely carries money! Good job someone else was organised or they might have had to wash up (that wasn't something Liz really wanted to do on holiday).

Was there any hope for Tina?

Was Liz going to survive Tina?

Oh well, back on with the rest of the day. One day Liz would get revenge, or would she...?

They then had to trek back to their room to reunite Tina with her lost purse before they could go any further. This was actively encouraged by Liz as shopping was on the agenda next.

The first point of call after this hiccup was to find the location where they had to meet for the trip later in the day. Due to Liz's insistence and organisation overload, luckily it wasn't too far from the main shopping area. Much to her relief, as she wouldn't have to drag Tina away from the shops too early.

It wasn't a particularly warm day, a bit cloudy and about fifteen degrees Celsius, but this didn't dampen their spirits.

The shops started to get very boring as they mostly sold the same type of souvenirs, but Tina still wanted to visit them all. This was another habit Liz had to get used to!

They got nearer to the pier area and wandered around a small shopping complex until they spotted a Crepe shop – yum-yum. Lunch was calling and they had the most amazing banana and chocolate crepe each. With full bellies, Liz managed to steer Tina back to the meeting point, which was a bit like a tourist information office; carefully guiding her past the shops, which wasn't an easy task.

Tina announced that they had loads of time before they had to be there, but, as Liz likes to be early everywhere, she managed to lead Tina past the shops.

At last Liz spotted the office they needed to be at. Tina then noticed a Harley Davidson shop opposite. As she disappeared in there, Liz thought she would just go and check the status of the trip for later as they were a bit early. After speaking to a man in the office, she was told that they weren't booked onto the evening trip and they had stopped doing them anyway. Panic ensued as this was a highlight for both of them and, after some convincing, the man said he would give them a lift down to the pier and they could catch the next ferry, which was leaving in fifteen minutes. He gave Liz a voucher to get on it, which would compensate for missing the evening trip.

Meanwhile, Tina was oblivious to this as she was still in the shop across the road. So after a mad dash run by Liz to cross the road, she retrieved her, spouting garbled instructions and the story about a cock up somewhere. Liz pushed Tina into the car, as she was objecting due to the fact that this wasn't the trip they booked.

Although she was right about that, Liz had been told that if they missed this ferry there wasn't another one that day; so it was either this or nothing. So Tina was told to be quiet, stop moaning and just get on with it, otherwise they would miss it. This fell on deaf ears as Tina continued to hurl a barrage of abuse at the poor man taking them to the pier.

After almost dragging Tina off the man, Liz got her into the queue for the ferry. After she realised that they were given the incorrect pier number and a quick run around to find the right place. Tina was still moaning about it. Liz hoped this wouldn't last as she knew Tina was desperate to see Alcatraz, as much as she was.

The Ferry was boarded, and once it set off Tina calmed

down a bit. She realised that she was on the way and nothing she could do now was going to change the fact that they were not going to get on that evening ferry to see the island in the dark.

After what seemed like a very quick journey, the next thing they knew, they were landing on Alcatraz. The views from the ferry were amazing. They watched the island getting closer, and the Golden Gate Bridge getting further away; the skyline from the city was an enviable sight.

The first thing they saw when they got off the ferry was the exercise ground used by prisoners. Then they walked on and up a steep hill to enter into the building at the top. They were mesmerised with the whole place from the minute they stepped off the ferry. It was so eerie, and they were very disappointed not to be able to go on the evening tour. But never mind, a complaint would be sent later to the Tour Company they had used to book all the trips! Even Tina was happy now.

The ferries going back seemed to leave on a regular basis, so they knew that they could catch any ferry back until the last one, which was around five p.m. It was now around three p.m. so at least they had got there and could get a couple of hours to explore. In hindsight, this was not enough time and they could quite easily have spent all day there. It was fascinating.

They wandered around the buildings, taking it all in and watched a demonstration of how all the cell doors were opened and closed at the same time; listening intently to the sound of the cell locks and trying to imagine what it must have been like to be trapped behind these bars.

They also saw the cells from which the big escape happened and the holes that were dug through; along with the actual papier-mâché painted heads that were positioned at the end of the beds to make it look like the prisoners were still sleeping.

They went to the canteen, which had gas nozzles in the ceiling. In the event of a major disruption, they would have just gassed the prisoners, and the unfortunate prison wardens that happened to be supervising them at the time. There were so many things and they learnt so much about this island, they were hooked!

The shop on the island had lots of the usual tourist stuff, of which they did buy some items to take home. They were told that one of the prison wardens had written a book about his experiences and was available that day to meet and to sign his books so Liz bought one. But unfortunately they just missed him – due to the late arrival and the organiser's cock-up! It didn't stop her getting the book though, as this could be interesting reading later.

Time was getting on and they set off to walk down the hill to get to the ferry, which had a large queue waiting for it. Apparently the ferry could only take a certain number of people, then the rest had to wait for the next one. Luckily, they were the last ones onto this ferry, so at least they didn't have to stand in a queue for another half an hour.

They were exhausted already but there was still lots more to see today – Tina didn't realise at this time what Liz was planning later (could this be her revenge?).

Off the ferry they got, and they headed back to the Wharf area where they immediately went looking for dinner. Unfortunately for them, all the electrics were off all along Fisherman's Wharf, so no one could cook anything. They didn't fancy anything cold, so they decided to head inland where there was a chance the electric was still working, as suggested by some of the restaurant staff.

They set off walking up a street called Taylor Street and passed the trams heading off that way, which were full anyway. Liz wanted to walk to the top of the hill in the area where Bullitt was filmed. Tina hadn't realised this, which gave Liz a chuckle. Revenge after this morning loomed, she thought.

About halfway up the hill they found a diner that had lights on. Yippee, someone had electric!

This place had seating outside, so they went in and ordered pizzas and drinks, then sat outside just chilling and giving their feet a rest. They chatted to some locals sitting outside with them until they had eaten, then Liz persuaded Tina to walk a bit further. A bit further ended up right at the top of the hill, much to Tina's disgust. But the walk was worth it, as the view was breath-taking and they could see Alcatraz, too.

Now, how do they get back down to Fisherman's Wharf? There were some steps that went downhill and looked like they would lead through a park area. To cut a long story short, this was the route they decided to take, and they ended up in Chinatown.

"Great idea that was," said Tina in disgust, as she realised how much further they had to walk.

Tina soon calmed down as she discovered more shops selling t-shirts, etc. so they duly went into most of them. Liz was getting bored by this time, so she tried to coerce Tina with the promise of getting back to the hotel and taking her shoes off.

On the way they passed an interesting looking place that did Chinese buffet and Tina was desperate to try some authentic cuisine. Liz, being a vegetarian, would struggle but she reluctantly agreed to keep the peace and keep Tina's mind off her feet. Anything for a peaceful life.

They went in and were directed to a table in the corner, so they were sitting diagonally, facing each other, and with Tina facing the entrance. She always liked to see who comes and goes and loved a bit of people watching. Although, by this point, they were the only ones in the restaurant so had the full attention of the waiters.

Even though it wasn't too long ago that they ate, it didn't stop them eating again. After all, sometimes they never knew when they were going to eat again.

Whilst Liz was checking her map and looking for the quickest route back to their hotel. Tina seemed to be transfixed on something on the other side of the window, out on the street. Liz turned round to see what was so fascinating.

There was a group of Chinese men, all in white t-shirts, lurking around outside on the pavement.

Liz said, "I wonder what that's all about?"

Tina replied, "They are looking a bit angry to me."

Oh great, not another load of trouble.

Liz said, laughing, "You had better get out there and sort them out then."

To which Tina replied that there was no chance of that! Liz thought that was unusual as Tina is always the first one to get herself into a confrontational situation, so she turned round to take a better look.

The group had gotten larger, and they seemed to all be carrying something in their hands, but it wasn't guns. Upon closer scrutiny, they seemed to be holding some sort of long baseball bats and they started chanting and shouting across the street.

Tina said, "Oh shit, there is going to be a fight. I bet they are part of a gang, and we are going to get caught up in the middle of gang warfare."

"Don't be ridiculous," said Liz, thinking that Tina's imagination was back on overtime again.

Liz turned round again, just to check, as she knew what Tina's imagination was like, so she didn't take her seriously.

"Holy shit," said Liz, noticing another group over the road wearing black t-shirts, thinking that for once Tina might be right.

The waiters seemed to be getting very agitated and appeared to be wanting them to leave, so Liz paid the bill. Then they got up from their seats, picked up their bags, and put on their jackets to leave.

Suddenly, one of the waiters came over to them and rattled on in Chinese. Liz and Tina had no idea what he was on about, but he was very frightened.

Eventually they realised that he wanted them to leave by the back door as he didn't want to draw any more attention to the restaurant by having customers walk into the crowd that was slowly building outside.

He grabbed their arms and, glancing behind him, he pulled them into the kitchen at the back. Liz and Tina were looking at each other and both were wondering what he was going to do with them. The waiter's fear was getting passed onto them now.

He ushered them through the empty kitchen and into a kind of entrance hall at the back that had stairs to the right and a door to the left. He opened the external door, then went first and looked outside from left to right. He then told them to go, in a very urgent manner, which freaked Liz out a bit and even

Tina looked worried.

They stepped outside into a grubby looking alley. The sort of place you wouldn't venture down during the day unless it was an emergency. Oh, but wait, it was an emergency!

The waiter pointed to the right, so they went in that direction, leaving him to run back inside and bolt the door in a hundred places. They were now on their own in a back alley, with no idea where they were, or even which way they should be going.

"Fuck, fuck, fuck," said Tina.

"Well, that's not helpful, Tina," replied Liz, wondering what they should do next.

The sound of chanting and shouting was still close.

Liz said, "Maybe we should go the opposite direction of all the noise and that way we might just get out of here in one piece."

Liz just set off walking, leaving Tina to follow very close behind. The alley they were in led them out into the street next to the one where the gangs were. The problem was that they needed to go into that street to get back to the hotel.

So Liz said, "Right, we are going the long way round. There is no way we are walking that way."

Tina moaned again about her aching feet and was told to be quiet as they had more important things to worry about than her feet!

Continuing on their route, they ended up back near the pier area, so it wasn't too far to the hotel. Well, maybe a bit more of a walk. The end was in sight, but Tina moaned so much about her feet, she actually ended up taking her shoes off and walking barefoot – still moaning!

Lots of walking later, and a few missed turns, they made

it back to their hotel room – phew! After checking the number of steps they had walked, Liz announced that throughout the day they had walked around twenty-five thousand steps – no wonder they had sore feet.

Liz looked on the local news on the internet to find that it was some triad gang causing a bit of trouble with some rivals. They were damn lucky to escape that load of trouble. Goodness knows what would have happened if they had walked out into that lot!

After getting showered and trying to calm themselves down, it was time to start packing again for the next morning. They would be leaving San Francisco and heading off to goodness knows where, as each day on the bikes was all merging together and they were starting to get confused about where they were.

Back to the normal routine of setting the alarm for six a.m. A bit of a shock after a day off, but they could have easily spent a few days in San Francisco, as they both loved the place, but there was another day in the saddle tomorrow to look forward to (sigh) as they drifted off to sleep.

Note to selves – if they ever visit again, they were going to be very much on their guard next time.

Chapter 17
Day 11 San Francisco to Monterey

SAN FRANCISCO TO MONTEREY, ONE HUNDRED
AND EIGHTEEN MILES

Today's plan was to get to Monterey before nightfall. At the
morning meeting they were all told that it was only about one
hundred and eighteen miles. Great news for them as they
thought they can do that easy-peasy, after what they have been
used to! The route was to take them over the Golden Gate
Bridge and back again (that is not the right direction, but you
can't visit this city without going over the bridge).

They all revved up the bikes and set off by eight a.m. as
normal. They were all bunched up together as they were told
that they have to stay in a tight group in the cities, because if
one bike gets separated, then it would take most of the day
finding them again. The weather was cold and cloudy, so, yet
again, they were padded out with more layers.

On the way, Don pulled them all over and explained about
a famous street called Lombard Street that a lot of people like
to ride down and also suggested an alternative route for those
less confident on the very windy hill. Everyone got ready to
set off and the group split slightly as Liz decided she wasn't
going to tackle it. She would go the longer route to the bottom.
When she stopped, she noticed that Tina was behind her. She
asked Tina why she hadn't gone with everyone else.

Tina just said, "I was following you."

Then, when she realised she had missed out on the fun

hill, she was gutted.

"Serves you right for not listening," Liz said.

As they made their approach to the bridge, they were in awe of this grand structure and couldn't quite believe they were actually going to ride over it. This was a true experience that would probably never happen again. They tried to make the most of it, but this proved to be harder than it looked. They were so busy concentrating on where they are going, and staying together, that they felt they missed out a bit on the experience. Maybe one day they would go back and next time they would walk over it instead.

They were led to a lay-by not far off the bridge on the other side, where everyone stopped for photo opportunities with the bridge in the background. It then became apparent that they had lost a bike somewhere, so the leader had to go back and find them – broken down!

Luckily, a spare bike was on a trailer being towed by the minibus, which held all the luggage (this followed everywhere as a support vehicle). But it seemed to take ages to get to the position where they could all set off together again. Everyone was getting frozen, sitting around without any information about what was happening, so everyone was getting very fed up – so much for an easy day, they were behind in time already and there was no café in sight to appease with coffee and cake.

At last they were on the move, hopefully to warmer climes – how wrong could they be.

Back over the bridge and off they went, thinking they were going to be riding down the coast, wrong again! They kept going and ended up on the road from hell through a forest. It was raining, very cold and foggy, and the road had lots of twists and turns. Which on a sunny day would be a great biking road, but in the rain it was horrific. They were cold, hungry, tired, and fed up (understatement of the day).

At last they were allowed to stop for lunch at a place called Alice's Restaurant, in the middle of nowhere. They all got settled inside and, after some wait and attracting the attention of a waitress, they ordered hot food and hot drinks, which seemed to take ages to arrive. They were concerned they would miss out on lunch again due to the tight schedule.

Lunch arrived and Tina had to send her meat back as it was undercooked. They also served Liz with the incorrect order, so she had to wait for them to cook her the correct one, which all took so much time. It was hurried and they didn't have time to finish it anyway as back on the bikes they went again.

This time they were heading to the freeway and Highway One, hoping to see some civilisation soon and warmth!

As Liz and Tina liked to stay at the back of the group, they found that they got separated during a particular session of overtaking on the freeway; due to cars trying to slot in between them. They rode the bikes as fast as they dared (what was the speed limit? No idea!), but they still couldn't catch up. The group seemed quite happy to leave them behind – maybe they were trying to tell them something. Luckily for them, the support vehicle always followed the last bike, and he overtook them and led them to the hotel. If it hadn't been for him they would have continued on the freeway and ended up in a completely different place – just their luck, anyway!

Tina had taken her gloves off whilst on the freeway (no one never knew why!) but she decided to sit on them for safety. That was when one of them escaped her clutches and ended up in the middle of the road, so she was gutted as they were her favourite gloves. Typical Tina.

Meanwhile back at the hotel, after getting parked up next

to everyone else who had already arrived and checked in, Liz found a luggage trolley for their six cases and got their room key.

Another nice room and a bed each. They had stayed in some lovely hotels on this trip and great news to get separate beds, too. At this point they had started to get used to living out of suitcases and not knowing where on earth they were anymore. All they knew was that they were hungry and tired, so they went out to find food.

They ended up at an Italian restaurant, which served nice cold beers. Tina kept bothering the poor young lad, who got the short straw to serve them, by insisting on chatting to him. He was very polite and did try to make his getaway without appearing rude, which is not easy once Tina has decided to converse.

They had a walk about to explore the small town after their meal, so at least they could get chance to see the town they were staying in before they went back to the hotel. They were still suffering with sore feet from yesterday, too, so they were ready for bed. The only thing they wanted to do was get changed into their pyjamas and chill out for a bit, but the next thing they knew the room phone rang – very strange, they thought, who would be ringing them?

Hotel Reception – they had received a complaint about their room being noisy and would they please be quiet! They were too tired to make any noise, so were shocked to say the least. Oh well, bedtime calls. At least they couldn't get told off for sleeping.

Actual mileage today – one hundred and fifty.

Stayed at the Hotel Abrego, in Monterey, for one night.

Chapter 18
Day 12 Monterey to Pismo Beach

MONTEREY TO PISMO BEACH, ONE HUNDRED AND
FIFTY-TWO MILES

They woke up to another cloudy day. They had thought this
was supposed to be the sunshine state, but they had yet to see
much sun! It just seemed to be cold all the time, a bit like being
at home really.

Time to get motivated for the day and, at this point in the
trip, they were starting to dream about the end. This wasn't
good news after all the planning and cost that had gone into
this so-called holiday. A holiday it definitely was not, but
hopefully they would look back on this and have fond
memories of their 'adventure'.

They had to keep washing all the long-sleeved tops, as
they were wearing four layers most days due to the cold. So,
another rummage around their cases and repacking again.
They were so tired that Liz ended up putting her pants on
inside out – who cares anyway!

Off they go again, the sound of all the Harleys starting up
always gave them a shiver of excitement every morning (until
they realised what else was in store).

Today they were all told they were going to do one
hundred and fifty-two miles, which sounds not a lot of miles
but by the time they stopped for petrol (which isn't easy, due
to the number of bikes to get filled up), and a couple of coffee

breaks and lunch, suddenly it seemed a long day.

They stopped at a ranch and park area for lunch, but they now knew there wasn't much time allocated for food. They decided to just get snacks. Tina got in a queue for hot dogs and, as usual, there were hardly any vegetarian options for Liz, so she settled for a large piece of carrot cake and a nice cup of tea – heaven!

This ride was taking them south on Highway 101, with the beach in view almost all the way. This scenery was starting to look fantastic. It's just a shame they had to spend so much time concentrating on the road and making sure they didn't get left behind that they really didn't get the chance to take it all in and enjoy it.

They were thrilled when the leader pulled into a lay-by, or car park area, next to the beach and said they could have a few minutes there to see the seals. They all walked across to watch them wallowing on the beach and one of the volunteers was on hand to talk about them. They were told that they were on live cam, so they decided to check this out when they got home. They only got to chat to her for a few minutes, but she was so knowledgeable and enthusiastic about the seals it was hard to leave. But, sure enough, they got dragged away and back to the bikes. Another short stop.

Back onto the bikes and, as usual, the sound of all the bikes starting up was still giving them a buzz; until reality hit, and it was back to the hard slog of heading to the next hotel. It seemed like a long way, but at least it was the coast road, even though the pace was quite quick. It was a shame really, as it would have been nice to be at a more leisurely pace so that everyone could enjoy the scenery.

They managed to keep up with the pack and, as usual,

stayed at the back. At least that way they could slow a bit to have a look around, then speed up to catch the group without causing a problem to the other bikes, who might have been behind them.

The time seemed to pass a bit quicker and before they knew it they had arrived at their next hotel, a bit early. This was great news as it was nice not to have to be rushed.

Once all the bikes were secured and they had got checked in and showered, they felt clean and human again. They decided to go out and find food. It was a nice, small town and they found a nice restaurant that had some live folk music going on. They ate in there, then decided to explore the town a bit.

Tina stopped a couple in the street and asked them what day it was. They had been getting confused with the days, but Liz hadn't realised Tina was completely lost (in her head!).

They stayed at the Sandcastle Inn, Pismo Beach for one night.

Chapter 19
Day 13 Pismo Beach to Los Angeles

PISMO BEACH TO LOS ANGELES, TWO HUNDRED AND TWENTY-FIVE MILES

Another early start at six a.m. Today was the last full day on the bikes and they were really looking forward to having a few days off before they went home, but they were kind of sad that they were coming to the end of the road.

They start the day with more struggles, with packing and tiredness. Tina got out of bed, put her neck roll on, and wandered around the room aimlessly. Liz asked if she was going to wear anything else today, as it would be best if she put more clothes on – wearing only a neck roll might get a few looks!

"Oh shit, I think I packed everything else," pronounced Tina.

She then had to find enough clean clothes to wear, and Liz managed to persuade her to get dressed as this was the last six a.m. morning – yippee!

It was to be a long day, two hundred and twenty-five miles long to be exact. At the morning meeting they were all told that they had to stay bunched up, especially as they got closer to Los Angeles, due to the number of lanes on the drive into the city. If anyone got lost, they would more than likely stay lost as the chances of locating them were slim.

Positive start, then!

The bikes rolled away for the last time, and back onto the road again. They stopped for lunch opposite a beach, at a fish and chip restaurant which had very slow service due to the sheer numbers in passing trade they got. So they only just managed to finish their lunch before they were all rushed off again. They really wanted to get onto the beach opposite, but no such luck as the leader ensured they all kept moving.

The next stop, and the last one before they started entering the city, was at Malibu Beach, for some photographs. No time for a look around though, as they were off again on the last leg of the journey.

The lanes into Los Angeles were quite mesmerising. They had never seen traffic like this before, but they had to concentrate with staying in a tight group as no one wanted to get left behind, they swapped back and forth between lanes and traffic. Fifteen bikes trying to keep together throughout this part of the journey was not easy, but they all made it safely to the Harley Davidson meeting point.

They parked the bikes up and had to stay with the bikes whilst someone came round and checked them all. They needed that piece of paper to show there wasn't any damage. Surprisingly enough, there wasn't.

They got their bikes unloaded, although they only really had a rucksack and a few things in the panniers, then they went into the shop for a look around. Tina bought some long-sleeved t-shirts to take home, then they were ushered into a minibus (another rush around) to be taken to the hotel, which was by the airport.

After checking in, they were given an hour to get ready for the party night. They were told that if they were not in the hotel lobby by six-thirty, they would be left behind.

"Oh no, that means rushing Tina," thought Liz, "How is that going to work as it takes an hour for her to put her face on without doing anything else, this was to be a challenge."

Sure enough, it was a challenge. Tina had no concept of time, so it took all Liz's powers of persuasion to get her organised and out of the door, and just in time as it happened.

Everyone piled into two minibuses and after about a ten-minute ride they were deposited at a bike shop and told that they would come back for them at eleven p.m. This seemed weird. Where had they been left?

After entering the shop, it all became apparent. There was a live band playing, plenty of beer and wine available, and a BBQ on the go – all just for the group! Fantastic!

Everyone tucked in and they could all relax at last and have a few beers and a chat. Although Tina didn't drink wine or beer, she ended up on cola instead (she only drinks Archers, which is a bit in limited supply here).

For some reason, Tina ended up getting up on the stage and singing (and this was without any alcohol). The band members just carried on playing and a fun night was had by all. It was a relief not to have to rush anywhere or worry about drinking too much and feeling ill the next morning before facing a long ride. That would have been nearly impossible.

The minibuses arrived on time and ferried everyone back to the hotel. Some went straight to the bar and carried on drinking, they were probably making up for lost time. Some were getting a flight the next morning, too.

Stayed at the Marriot Hotel, Los Angeles Airport, for one night.

Chapter 20
Day 14 Los Angeles Airport to Beverley Hills

Liz woke with a bit of a headache and longed to keep her head on the pillow for just a few more hours. No such luck, as they were on a deadline to check out.

A big fat struggle ensued to get out of bed and dressed (Tina had to put her face on first, though, to look a bit presentable) and off they went for breakfast. Everyone else they saw in the restaurant were a bit quiet and pale, and some didn't even make it downstairs! Obviously they all had a good night.

On the way back to their room they stopped at reception to enquire whether they could leave all their cases there until they had collected the hire car and returned to the hotel. Luckily, they were very accommodating so off they went to get the packing finished. After today they would be in the same hotel for five nights – no more unpacking and packing, yippee!

The hotel concierge had said that they could get a shuttle bus to the airport from the hotel. This sounded like a great plan. Of course, they got on it and ended up getting off at the wrong place, as the driver announced which terminal they were at each stop he made. They didn't know which stop they wanted so they took potluck.

They then had to go into the airport to try and find out which stop they should be looking for to get to the car rental site. There were some very helpful people in there that gave some advice, but it sounded a bit complicated. Never mind, they would just have to keep checking out each stop.

At last the driver announced that he was stopping at the car rental site. They were relieved to see the Avis rental building, where they were picking the hire car up from. They had to get in a large queue as there were so many people wanting hire cars. But the staff were very efficient and they soon had the keys to their car, with instructions as to which number it was parked at. They still didn't really know what they were looking for and had to double take when they saw their car – wow! They had the use of a bright red Mustang.

Tina wanted to stand out and make sure everyone knew she was coming. This was the car for them!

They managed to get themselves into it. Although they had been riding on the opposite side of the road, somehow they still weren't used to going the wrong way on the roads. Tina was the designated driver and was too short to reach the pedals, so they had to get out of the car to try and reorganise the driver seat (they had to get the attention of one of the attendants as they couldn't work this one out). There was no way she was going to let Liz drive!

The car was an automatic, and that, along with driving on the opposite side of the road, proved to be extremely challenging for Tina.

Liz was in charge of the map and directions but, with Tina driving, they could end up anywhere!

A few kangaroo jumps later and they were away out of the car park. Now, how on earth do they get back to the hotel to collect the cases? Today was proving to be full of challenges.

A lot of the large hotels had signposts to them, and they also tried to remember what direction the hotel was in.

Unfortunately, it appeared that Tina didn't know the difference between her left and right, so every time Liz shouted 'next left', Tina would turn right. This got them into more of a muddle and Tina was getting stressed. Oh dear, tempers could be getting frayed here and they hadn't even got their cases yet.

After a few more wrong turns, and the car stalling in some tricky places, they spotted the hotel. Tina drove up to the entrance and Liz ran in to collect the trolley with all six cases on it. By the time she got outside Tina had the boot open ready to load. Another challenge completed, they thought, as they drove away from the hotel.

First they had better fill up with petrol. At the garage the labels were confusing, so they decided to get the one that said 'gas', as Tina had seen that in the movies – Liz wasn't convinced though, so Tina was threatened with sorting it out if they got the wrong fuel. They couldn't work the pumps, so Liz had to go into the garage, where she was told that you have to pay for your fuel first before you can access the pump. How was she to know how much fuel they needed? They replied that she would get a refund if she paid too much. Having no alternative, she went back to the car and told Tina, who filled the car up to the amount Liz had paid. They were too tired to mess about and just wanted to get on their way.

As they tried to exit the garage, they saw traffic lights everywhere and had no idea which direction or how to follow the light system. Apparently it was slightly different to theirs. Tina just decided to set off anyway and got Liz screaming in her ear to stop as she was driving the wrong way on a red light. Another panicky moment and Liz went white (again).

"Just put your foot down and let's get on the road," said Liz.

Tina was silent for once and did as she was told.

They had booked their next hotel in Beverly Hills, so they had to get onto a freeway to reach it. There were so many lanes on it they didn't know which one was which, and lots of turns that looked like they should get off. Which, of course, they did frequently and got lost many times. After much colourful language going on, they actually found the right slip road to get off the freeway.

At the end of the slip road they had to make a snap decision as to whether they went left or right to the hotel. It was like a dual carriageway, with hotels on each side, so they couldn't tell which side theirs would be on. So they took a left – wrong decision again! After a few U-turns (illegal, they thought, but after all they were silly old women and could use that as their defence if needed), they spotted the hotel.

They turned in and Liz jumped out and went to check in and get a car park pass. Then they parked round the back and, after dragging all the cases around, at last they located their room.

Twin double beds and a balcony – fantastic!

They then proceeded to unpack as they were staying here until they went home. They felt like they could actually settle a bit. After discovering loads of dirty washing, Tina decided to take it to the laundry room, which housed washers and dryers for the guests.

They scrambled around for all the change they could find, and she went off to put the first load in. After a few minutes she came back and said she needed more change – why? She had only put all the change and the clothes into a dryer instead of the washer! As they didn't have any more, they had to go to reception and get change, then Liz decided to go with her and supervise.

They took the opportunity to have a look around the hotel whilst they were waiting for the washing to finish. They found a pool and Jacuzzi near the bar, and they had a large screen by the pool to show movies on, daily. They had made a good choice as the hotel was faultless.

After collecting the clean washing they took it back to the room so they could hang it to dry on the balcony. Luckily, Liz had brought her travel washing line (super organised again). Clean pants at last!

They had a chill out on the beds and tried to find something to watch on TV, then got themselves showered and changed so they could head out for food. They were both starving at this point.

They had booked 'Room Only' at this hotel, so they thought they would look out for suitable breakfast diners whilst they were out. They left the car behind and had a walk around to explore and get their bearings.

There were a number of places to eat, but they settled on an Irish pub! There wasn't any Irish staff in there, but it looked just like a pub at home. So they propped themselves at the bar and ordered drinks and food, whilst chatting to the bar staff and locals. One of the locals was telling them about a cat watch site her friend had set up online and made them promise to check it out when they got home. Maybe they would fit in round here as everyone seemed a bit bonkers.

The food was typical pub grub type, with large portions. It was excellent food and they completely stuffed themselves, then had dessert, too. Not sure how they were going to waddle back to the hotel now.

Tiredness overcame them, so they peeled themselves off

the bar stools that had by now moulded round them and headed off back. On the way they passed a small supermarket, so they called in there and bought fruit, yoghurts, and drinks, etc. for breakfast. Yes, they were still thinking about food! It seemed that the whole trip evolved around food, but this could be because they never knew when they were going to eat again.

Back at the room they filled the fridge with the purchases and crashed out for the night, exhausted.

Stayed at the Garland Hotel, in Beverley Hills, for five nights.

Chapter 21
Day 15 Los Angeles

No rush this morning – fantastic!

Gone were the six a.m. alarms, now a distant memory. Breakfasting in pyjamas, what a luxury!

They still had a busy day planned, though, as there was lots to pack into their last few days. But at least they could go at their own pace now, which wasn't marching pace.

Whilst organising themselves to go out for more adventures, Tina realised that she had lost the remote control for her GoPro camera. She thought she had left it on the bike but, knowing Tina, it could be anywhere. Anyway, she insisted they go back to the Eagle Rider shop in Los Angeles where they had handed the bikes back, to check.

The car journey there was the start of what was normal for Liz. Tina insisted she turn off where she shouldn't, so a couple of hours later they arrived at the shop. No one was aware of finding this remote, which actually looked like a watch that she had fastened around the handlebars. Liz was convinced it had just fallen off. Tina was a bit clumsy, and she usually lost most things at some point.

They were really concerned and then offered to refund her the cost of it, so that made Tina happy. They saved the day for Liz.

They set off back to the car, with a map and high hopes for a relaxing day. The first point of call this morning was at a beauty parlour for a massage they had previously booked online. It wasn't too far from the hotel, so they had to endure the return journey to that area. Tina found a car park outside and dumped the car. They then registered with the receptionist, who gave them health forms to complete. Tina had requested a hard massage and Liz wanted a more gentle massage, so they duly ticked all the boxes and handed the forms back. After about ten minutes, they saw two ladies talking to the receptionist. One looked quite a bruiser, so Liz was hoping Tina got her! Nooooo, she collected Liz instead!

Just when Tina was saying, "I hope that one takes me as I need a hard massage."

They were taken to separate treatment rooms. They had really been looking forward to a full body massage to relax them from their trip, so they could start to wind down for the last few days.

An hour later, they appeared back in the reception area to complete the payments. The receptionist also wanted them to tip the masseurs. As Liz was in agony from her massage (she obviously got the one meant for Tina), she declined and Tina only gave a small tip. They were not happy with this, so they both had to make a quick escape back to the car as the receptionist was trying to explain that it is normal to tip and was getting a bit irritated.

They had planned to go into central LA, as Tina wanted to see the Walk of Fame. So Tina managed to drive there, with the help of her navigator, and park in a multi storey without too many problems, for a change.

Fascinated with star spotting on the pavement, they had soon walked quite a way and ended up falling for one of the old tricks of enlisting for a bus trip round the houses of the stars. Tina was very excited by this, but Liz was reluctant. She went anyway as Tina was so excited about going. Well, anything to keep the peace! In the end, it wasn't too bad as they got a tour of the area and also came back down Rodeo Drive, which they wouldn't have had time to visit independently.

Another tip was demanded by the bus driver. There was a notice above his seat giving a list of the recommended tips, which totalled around the same as the price of the tour. Needless to say, he didn't get it. They were starting to tip reluctantly as it was now taking a chunk out of their holiday money. They had saved for so long to get this far, they were not happy to keep giving it away (not that they didn't appreciate the service they had, which was all excellent, but enough was enough).

After managing to escape from the bus without leaving a large tip, they decided to wander down the Walk of Fame again, on the other side of the road, and do a bit of souvenir shopping.

Most of the shops all sold the same usual sort of souvenirs and in one of the shops they went into there was an old, chubby man who turned out to be a bit creepy. Once he realised they were English he followed them round the whole shop and kept trying to touch them on the bottom and put his arm round both of them. Time for a quick escape! Needless to say, nothing was purchased in that one.

They both bought a few T-shirts, in a different shop, then decided it was time for food. They headed back towards the car, looking for somewhere nice to eat.

As they were going through the shopping centre, on the way to the car park, Liz spotted a Tea Shoppe (not many of these round here), so she insisted on visiting it. Tina followed reluctantly.

After they sat down and spoke to the waiter, it became apparent that it actually didn't sell coffee, only tea (Tina was stumped now), so Liz was in her element as tea seemed to be quite rare round here! They ordered food, as well as tea for Liz, and Tina decided to try iced tea with hers, which she didn't like. The Tea Shoppe also had a wall full of shelves covered in tea pots for sale. Brilliant for Liz, as she ended up buying one! It would be a miracle if it got home in one piece though.

Back to the car and another adventure to find the hotel again. They still couldn't get the hang of these roads, even with maps!

Relieved as the hotel came into view, they got parked up. As soon as they got into their room they got their swimwear on, as Tina had spotted that the Jacuzzi was still open. They got into it and the nice warm water felt so good. Then Tina noticed that Liz's back was covered in bruises – this was only from her so-called relaxing massage earlier in the day, it was damn sore!

Shock over, Tina started chatting to some Australians in the Jacuzzi, who were staying at the hotel (whilst Liz was still reeling from her bruising session), and, with drinks in hand and a movie playing, they eventually started to relax.

Another big day loomed tomorrow. This holiday business was so exhausting.

Chapter 22
Day 16 Universal Studios

Back to an early start, as they were going to catch the free shuttle from the hotel to Universal Studios which left at nine a.m. – this was still a lay-in though!

They checked out the room fridge to see what was left for breakfast. Only fruit, but better than nothing. So, after a quick rush around and a long wait for Tina to put her face on for the day, they eventually managed to make it to the bus.

It was only a short ride to Universal Studios. They had originally booked to go to SeaWorld, but the trip was cancelled two days before and, as the refund came back in immediately, they decided to book this trip instead. It was a bit of a last-minute decision.

After chatting to some other tourists in the jacuzzi the previous night, who had been that day and who had suggested that it was best to do the tour first (as the queue's get really bad later), for once they decided to follow someone's advice. They headed for the bus tour start to get in the queue, which had already started to form. This proved to be a good decision.

The tour was very interesting, then got a bit scary when they met King Kong and the bus started getting thrown about. Liz wanted to get off at this point, although Tina was loving it.

After praying for the end, Liz was relieved to get back to the drop off point and get her feet back on solid ground. Also, food was calling.

As they were walking round, a bronze-coloured statue suddenly started dancing. The next thing Liz knew, Tina had gone off and started dancing with him, to the cheers of everyone else.

"Now, where to hide round here?" thought Liz.

Embarrassment over, Liz managed to drag Tina away to go and find something to eat. This proved quite tricky for a vegetarian, so they had to resort to some sort of sandwich.

All this walking around was getting very tiring, when they were already exhausted from their 'holiday', so they decided to meander towards the exit. Although, in reality, they ended up going round in circles until they spotted a bar. So they went in there for a drink and a sit down.

Opposite the bar was a Minions ride, which Tina kept eyeing up. Liz encouraged her to go and see if she could get on it as, if you were on your own, you didn't have to join the queue. She got straight onto it. Liz sat back and relaxed with her drink. Phew, a bit of peace for ten minutes!

The ten minutes peace seemed to go on forever, not that Liz was complaining, but eventually she finished her drink and thought she had better go and find Tina. She was probably talking to someone who needed rescuing.

She went to the entrance and had a look around that area. Liz asked if there was a different exit, but the girl at the entrance said that everyone should come out the same way they went in. She described Tina to her and the girl remembered her coming in as she was on her own, but she couldn't remember her coming out again.

Liz tried to ring Tina, but no answer. That wasn't unusual, as she hardly ever answered her phone anyway. Then Liz realised it was in the bag that Tina had left her for safekeeping.

Now what should she do? She could hardly go to the Lost Children stand, tempting though it was.

There was nothing else for it. She would have to follow her onto the ride and see if she could find her in there, probably tormenting someone.

"I am going to kill her if I find her busy talking and making me come in after her," muttered Liz to herself.

Liz went in and had to sit down in a kind of cinema, then she had to sit through a short film. She found this so boring.

Then another film started. It was like a pretend roller coaster, where the film moved but you sat still in your seats. Hating these sort of rides, she closed her eyes, cursing Tina the whole time.

At least it didn't last long. Feeling a bit sick and disorientated, she got up from her seat and had a good look around when the lights came on, but one of the members of staff was ushering everyone out really quickly into the gift shop as they wanted to let the next group in.

Liz still couldn't see Tina anywhere. She must be in the gift shop, she thought, as Tina was drawn to any available shop. But you could only get in there if you went through the ride first.

The gift shop was quite busy as Liz sauntered out at the back of the group so she could get a good look around. As Tina was shorter than her, she wasn't easy to spot. Liz's best chance was to hear her, as she had a loud voice that carries everywhere.

Straining her ears, Liz was still unable to hear Tina anywhere, but it was quite bustling and noisy in the shop. Where the hell had she gone? Liz was fuming by this time.

Unsure of what to do and where to look next, Liz went

over to one of the shop assistants and showed her a photo of Tina on her phone. Liz asked her if she had seen anyone of that description. She looked puzzled and said she couldn't remember as they see so many faces every day.

Once Liz mentioned that they were English and that Tina was quite loud, the penny dropped.

She said, "Oh yes, one of the other assistants has taken her into the back of the shop to the storeroom."

But she wasn't sure why.

Liz got the directions for the storeroom and headed over there, stamping her feet and fuming.

She went through a door that was marked 'Private', which led into a short corridor. From there she could just follow the noise that was Tina's voice, which took her into another room full of shelves with a small staff kitchen in the corner.

There was Tina, having a coffee with one of the male shop assistants, talking about bikes. The shop assistant was showing her photos of his bike and Tina was telling him about the adventures they had been through to get this far.

Liz stormed over to Tina.

"Have you been in here all this time?" she asked.

Tina replied, "Oh, yes. I just got talking to this nice young man and told him what we had been doing, so he wanted to show me pictures of his biking adventures whilst he was on his break."

"For fucks sake, you have been gone almost two hours and I have been looking everywhere for you. I even had to endure that stupid kids ride and feel sick to find you," said Liz.

Tina just looked blankly at her and said that she hadn't realised how long she had been gone, and that Liz would be worried. With that, she got up off the stool and said goodbye to the shop assistant and duly followed Liz back out through the gift shop into the fresh air.

Liz was still fuming at losing a couple of hours, whilst Tina, who had no concept of time, couldn't understand the fuss.

"Right, we had better get back to the shuttle bus and do NOT go anywhere else on your own talking for hours," said Liz.

So they now had to try and find their way out to the bus stop to get back to the hotel. Luckily Liz remembered which stop it was once they had made it out of the park.

All Liz could think about on the way back was getting back in that jacuzzi with a drink and watching a film on the outdoor screen, which didn't last long before Tina got bored.

Tina then asked Liz what she fancied doing that evening. Liz replied that they could go into LA at night to see it all lit up.

"We can't do that," said Tina.

"Why ever not?" asked Liz.

"Well, we might bump into some undesirable characters or even the Chippendale wannabes."

Liz replied, "Get the car keys then."

Tina realised what she had said and grabbed her bag quick. They were out of there and on their way before they knew what had happened.

After arriving on Hollywood Boulevard, they wandered up and down the street, still amazed by the stars in the pavement. They always seemed to find one they hadn't found before.

Unfortunately, Tina wasn't looking where she was going as her eyes were glued to the floor, fascinated by the stars, so she kept bumping into people. Liz had to keep apologising for her, then got hold of her and told her to stay upright and stop messing about, much to the amusement of passers-by. She felt like she was taking a child out.

No sign of the Chippendales, so back to the hotel.

Chapter 23
Day 17 San Diego

A lovely lay-in awaited, so they took full advantage. The exhaustion was catching up with them but they had to keep going as they had planned to head to San Diego today. They were really looking forward to this as they had heard so much about it.

Although the thought of a hair-raising ride with Tina driving slightly unnerved Liz a bit – guess they would get lost again, this seemed to be getting a habit.

After dragging themselves up and having breakfast, they were delayed by another hour due to Tina putting her face on, but they eventually hit the road.

What a scary drive on the way there. Getting out of LA was always going to be difficult. The swopping lanes at the last minute, and Tina not knowing right from left, was sure to cause some nervous breakdowns.

At last they arrived in San Diego. Tina kept driving round in circles as they had planned to go to the harbour and park near there. After following the signs, they found a car park. Tina asked some women who were caught just getting into their car and they said they didn't know where the harbour was, neither did another man she asked. Very strange that no one seemed to have heard of it.

Obviously, they would drive around a bit more like any sensible people would and get lost a few times. Suddenly Tina spotted a space by the side of the road so they thought they would nip in there quick as, by this time, they were getting hungry and thirsty so were past caring about the parking issue.

After a wander around, they still couldn't find the harbour, but they did discover that it was a bank holiday that day so not much was open – great!

Luckily, some eateries were open so they got settled into the only place that served some vegetarian options, albeit full of cigar-smoking men, but hunger won out; they got fed and watered whilst planning their next move, which wasn't difficult as they could only head back because there was nothing to do round here.

Whilst they were discussing this, two women overheard them and came over. They sat themselves down next to them and started giving them some advice on where they could go.

These two women seemed to be getting a bit closer to them and then started to suggest that they all go back to their apartment. Tina then realised what was going on (these women were coming onto them), Liz, of course, had no idea, not being as streetwise as Tina.

Liz noticed Tina was starting to fidget and kept trying to catch her attention. This all fell on deaf ears as Liz was used to Tina doing strange things, but on this occasion, though, she would be forgiven.

Tina suggested that her and Liz should visit the ladies toilet first, so Liz duly followed her, thinking it was a good idea. Tina then announced what was happening to Liz. Liz went white and said that they had to get out of there quick. There was an open window in one of the cubicles, so they decided that this was their route out of there.

As Liz was taller, it was decided that she would go first,

then she could help Tina get through. Panicking in case they got stuck, Liz was so relieved that she had lost some weight before the trip as she managed to get through headfirst with a big push from Tina. She managed to support her fall with her hands. Then it was Tina's turn. Of course she just went through like a bull in a China shop, before Liz was ready for her, and landed in a big pile of mud. Looking like they had been in a fight, they sneaked out of the alley and made a run for it back to the car.

"Quick, get the car started," said Liz.

Tina couldn't find the keys in her bag, it seemed like forever before they were located. The car started straight away and Liz was shouting, "Go, go, go."

The wheels spun and they were off.

Getting out was slightly better than getting in, but towards LA. they got a bit lost again. They saw a sign for Long Beach, so Tina wanted to visit that. By this time it was dark so there was nothing to see, but she insisted so off they went. They drove through it and Tina wanted to stop. It looked like a very rough neighbourhood, so Liz was shouting to keep going and not to stop – nothing to look at anyway, but at least they had been.

On the way back, Tina decided she wanted to try and pick up a bottle of Archers to drink back in the room, so they stopped at four stores looking for any kind of peach schnapps. Nowhere had any and none really knew what she was talking about. They ended up buying some Baileys and Malibu to take back instead.

They got back in the car and headed back to find the hotel. Another adventure in getting lost and those drinks were starting to look very welcome.

They got onto the freeway and suddenly the car boot popped open, because Tina had been playing with the gadgets and had pressed a button with no idea what it was for. Liz panicked a bit, so Tina pulled up by the side of the freeway, in the dark, to close the boot – all that could be seen were car lights flying past them and lots of horns beeping; if they ever got out of this place without getting into any sort of trouble, it would be a miracle!

By nine forty-five p.m., they got back to the hotel, so it was straight into the room, swimming costumes on, and into the Jacuzzi outside with some drinks. The hotel were still running films on the big screen so at last it was a chance to relax for a bit after a long and stressful day. Phew.

Chapter 24
Day 18 Warner Brothers and Los Angeles

Last full day today, so mixed feelings about leaving here, but they were ready to go home.

As they emerged from their beds and looked outside, it was cloudy (again). The forecast was going to reach twenty-two degrees today – they were getting fed up with being cold! Still no colour on either of them, so it didn't look like they had left their front door, very disappointing.

They had planned to go on a VIP Warner Bros tour today at one p.m., so at least they didn't have to rush for a change.

As they were getting ready, Tina wanted to charge her GoPro and discovered there was no memory left on her SD card as it had been recording all night in her bag – this could only happen to Tina.

Oh well, they had better get out for some breakfast and, bored with the same places, Liz thought they could try a different café, where they both had omelettes. Unfortunately, Tina found a long, black hair in hers, so she was nearly sick, and it completely put them both off their breakfasts. After complaining, they weren't really interested and didn't offer anything else or any refund, so they soon left; still hungry.

Right, map time again. Liz got her head into the map whilst Tina brought the car round. The number of lanes on the freeway confused them every time. It was always the same question, 'Do we get onto the lanes before the bridge or after?'.

They need to be right on this one, so as Liz shouts left, Tina goes right – what a start to the day! Oh well, at least they have seen another part of LA, even though they didn't want to!

Eventually they arrive at the studio and check in for the tour. They are taken into a small cinema with a number of other visitors to watch a short film on Warner Bros. They were then all allocated a tour guide, who escorted them to a small buggy, which took around six people. Once all six of them had been safely loaded onto the buggy, they set off.

The other four women on the tour were Americans, so they knew all the programmes the guide was telling them about. Neither Liz nor Tina had an idea of most of them. They were then shown a New York Street and Central Park, along with other streets of varying nationalities, including Paris and an Eastern European city.

They stopped and were taken into a house that had been on some TV show – they had no idea which show – but there was no upstairs in this house and apparently they change all the walls and décor for each TV programme it is used for.

The next stop was to go into a studio where another famous TV sitcom was filmed – again, they had no idea which one as neither of them watched any. It was like a small theatre, but it had cameras overhead, so it could be filmed with an audience and there were two sets next to each other, one being a café and the other one a kitchen.

Back onto the buggy and the next stop was into a two-storey warehouse. The downstairs was full of Batman memorabilia, including working cars and bikes, along with other items used in the films. Well at least they had heard of these, so it was much more interesting.

The upstairs was dedicated to Harry Potter – they had to

admit that neither of them had seen these, although it was still very fascinating, and the guide was certainly knowledgeable.

The most interesting stop for them was the prop warehouse. The whole area covered two hundred thousand square feet – enormous! It held more than four hundred and fifty thousand items, so obviously they couldn't see it all.

They were all taken through the lighting area, which just looked like a lighting shop. Lots of items were tagged with programme or film names, as they had been chosen and booked out for either an upcoming programme or film.

The tour ended in the gift shop (where all tours end). They managed to get themselves a drink and a snack before leaving to heading back to the hotel.

On their way back to the hotel, Liz had another brainwave.

"Why don't we go to one of those famous cemeteries as they look amazing, whilst we have some spare time?"

Tina looked at her and said, "Really," in a sarcastic tone.

"Oh yes, it will be interesting," said Liz.

After a few moans, Tina agreed, and they turned round and headed back into LA to the Hollywood Forever Cemetery. Of course, they followed the directions from Liz to ensure they found the right place.

They went past it a few times as it didn't really look like a cemetery, more like a park. Once they realised it was the right place, they drove in and found a parking space. Tina insisted on taking her GoPro to film their walking tour around the graves.

"Well, this is a weird way to spend a holiday," moaned Tina.

"Oh shut up," said Liz. "And stop whinging."

Silence ensued, a rare event around Tina.

It was very quiet and peaceful around the graves, and they spent ages looking for famous names, which kept Tina occupied and interested. They walked round the large pond and stopped to watch the ducks. Liz tried to get close to the ducks and her foot slipped, so one leg fell into the pond. She had a soaking and moaned the rest of the way round about being wet and cold.

As they headed back to the car, there was a large black car parked up ahead in the distance, with blacked out windows and no one in sight. They wondered if it was someone famous who had come to visit a grave and pondered on who it might be.

Suddenly, Tina grabbed Liz's arm and pulled her onto the ground behind a large gravestone.

"What the fuck did you do that for," said Liz. "I am already wet and now I am dirty, too."

"Shh," said Tina.

Liz looked at her, completely confused and dazed.

"Look over there, by that black car," Tina said.

When she diverted her eyes towards the car, there was a man hovering around it looking very suspicious, wearing a rucksack, and he looked like he had a gun, too.

"This is scary," said Tina.

"How the hell can we get to our car now?" Liz hissed.

Not knowing what to do, they stayed glued to their spot. There was no one else in sight and they couldn't get to their car without showing themselves to the man with the gun, as well as the black car and its occupants.

Tina had never been so quiet, and Liz was frozen to the spot.

"Well, this never happens in Bedale," said Tina.

"What do you think is happening?" said Liz.

"Looks like a drug deal to me," Tina replied.

"Wow!" said Liz.

"Not sure whether to be scared or excited," she said.

They seemed to be hiding for ages and Tina started moaning about getting pins and needles, but they dared not move just yet. Goodness knows what could happen if they showed themselves now.

"We should have gone straight back to the hotel, then this would never have happened," moaned Tina.

"For fucks sake, Tina, stop going on about it. We can't change it now, so we just have to come up with a plan to get to the car," replied Liz.

All of a sudden, a car door opened and a large man got out, who looked like he was built like a shed. The other man approached him, and, at this point, the front car door opened. Another similar sized man got out like a flash and then patted down the man that had been waiting around and seized his gun before he could make a move.

Throughout their meeting, the man from the front seat continued to keep his eyes peeled around the cemetery, so they had to stay well hidden.

By this time, they were quite terrified and worried.

"How the hell are we going to get out of this one?" said Liz.

Tina was silent for a nano-second, then said, "How the hell should I know!"

"Well, you are the streetwise one," replied Liz.

The bickering continued whilst they watched from behind the gravestone. They decided that all they could do was wait until they had gone. Which could be ages yet, they thought.

After what seemed like a long time, the man that had

gotten out of the back of the car reached into the place he had emerged from and handed a package to the man that was on foot. After sniffing and inspecting it, he took his rucksack off and opened it up to bring out a package to give back to the large man in exchange. He passed it to someone in the car and a few minutes later, after a conversation with the man inside, he climbed back into the car, along with the man from the front seat.

They looked around them, as it was still quiet, then closed the car doors and sped off with a squeal of the tyres.

The man with the rucksack also looked around and started walking away from that spot.

"Fucking hell," said Liz. "That man is heading our way."

"Oh shit," said Tina.

They got themselves together and edged around the gravestone as the man approached; so that they kept out of sight as he walked past. Luckily, he was looking straight ahead along the path not at the gravestones, otherwise he might have spotted them.

As they had gone full circle round the gravestone, not taking their eyes off rucksack man, they noticed that he started running. As he was going in the other direction, Liz and Tina decided to make a run for it to their car.

"Get the keys in your hand ready," said Liz.

So Tina rummaged around in her bag to locate them.

"You better not have dropped them somewhere," said Liz.

"It's OK, I have found them," Tina replied.

At this point they took another look around and could just see the man, still running, further away in the distance, so they took their opportunity and raced to the car.

They jumped in the car and Tina started the engine

immediately.

"We need to get out of here now," she said, with a squeal of tyres and Liz staring at her.

"We are not in the movies, you know," Liz said to her.

Tina just laughed, although it was probably a release from fear.

They headed back to the way they came in, as it was both entrance and exit. Getting the right side of the road was a bit trickier, with Tina driving and in a panic at the same time.

As they pulled out onto the main road, they noticed a white car behind them that wasn't there when they were waiting to exit the cemetery.

Liz looked back and, to her horror, noticed that the person in the passenger side was rucksack man and he was pointing at their car.

"Err, Tina," she said. "I think you had better draw on your previous professional driving experiences."

"Why?" Tina asked.

"Get your bloody foot down and get us out of here, that car behind us has rucksack man in and he was pointing us out to the other man who is driving. I think he knows we saw him," said Liz.

Tina didn't look back. She set off and the force pinned Liz to her seat. By this time Liz had stopped moaning about being wet and cold as there were far more important things to worry about.

Tina continued as fast as she dare as neither of them knew the speed limits. Liz got her head down into the map to direct her towards their hotel, which was about eight miles away, so plenty of opportunity to shake off that car. If it was actually following them.

They kept focussed and Liz kept checking in the mirror. She told Tina to just concentrate on driving and that she would keep her eyes on the map and the white car, which appeared to be following them.

Fortunately there were plenty of lights around, so they managed to get over a few on green whilst the white car got stuck on red, thereby increasing the distance between them, but they were not out of the woods yet.

They got onto the Hollywood Freeway and increased their speed. Tina was driving like a lunatic.

"Oh shit, we are going to either crash, or get pulled over," said Liz.

Tina replied, "We won't crash, trust me."

Tina's favourite saying was 'trust me', so that immediately made Liz worry more.

The white car seemed to be further away in the distance, until it was out of sight. As they were driving a red car, and there were quite a few red cars on the freeway at the time, this gave them some comfort that rucksack man wouldn't be able to pick them out.

It was the thought of that gun that scared them more, as they were just not used to seeing them. Although, when it comes to it, Tina could tuck her skirt into her knickers and fight like a man, that's if she hadn't verbally scared them off before that.

They felt that they were getting to be masters at this getting back to the hotel, especially under pressure, as they turned off the freeway. The white car was nowhere to be seen, so they breathed a sigh of relief and drove into the hotel car park, still looking behind them as they were still a bit nervous.

"Can we stop at the bar on the way back to the room?" Liz asked. "I need a beer and quick."

Tina moaned as she didn't really drink much but she realised it wasn't worth disagreeing as Liz was going there anyway.

They sat down, still looking around them in case, by some fluke, rucksack man had managed to follow them this far. At least it was their last day so, after tomorrow, they would be long gone.

After their nerves had calmed down, they went back to their room as it was packing time. It was a bit of a dash around to get all six cases packed (three each), then, as hunger set in, they managed to find some yoghurts and fruit they had kept for breakfast. They greedily polished them off as they didn't fancy going back out there again that night.

They were feeling a bit sad but were relieved after the things that had happened to them. No one was ever going to believe their stories when they got home.

Chapter 25
Day 19 Los Angeles to London Heathrow and HOME

They woke up feeling a bit strange as, after almost three weeks of being away and 'on the road', they would be taking their last journey to start the long trip home.

After a good sweep round of the room to check nothing had been left behind, they got checked out and the car loaded up. More map reading, too. Surely it wouldn't be difficult to get to the airport as it was big enough.

Getting to the airport wasn't too stressful. The worst bit was where the hell do they find the right car rental place to take the car back, it was like a maze.

Much later... they arrived at the airport from the shuttle bus that left from the car rental area.

The bus dropped them off in the wrong place, so they had to drag all their stuff around to find the correct check-in area, but, once they spotted it, they found they were too early – for a change.

It must be time for food. There was nothing in the part of the airport they were in, so they dragged their luggage across the road and walked for a while to find a café, to get fed and watered and ready to face the final leg of the 'holiday'.

Back to the check-in area and they managed to be at the front of the Premium Economy check-in. Luckily, they were allowed two cases in the hold and two bags on the flight as they had so much to carry.

Whilst they were waiting, Liz asked Tina what she had in her hand luggage. It seemed she had all her makeup, etc. After being told she couldn't take them on the flight, she had to open all her cases and repack them to move everything around. By this time she was getting very stressed so, luckily, they didn't have to wait too long to check-in and get rid of all the luggage.

Although the queue behind them was getting longer, and everyone was staring at them with all the cases open, they were probably worried that Tina was holding the queue up, although it almost came to that.

They both thought that LA airport would have loads of shopping and be a great place to wait, but they were very wrong. They were doing a lot of alterations, so there was very limited access to anything.

After a wander around the few shops available, they bought some perfume each and headed into the next shop.

This particular shop sold all sorts of knick-knacks and Tina saw a glass bauble with a decoration inside. She pointed out that this would be nice to take back for one of her grandchildren. Liz told her that it didn't look suitable for a young child.

To which Tina replied, "Well, it's only plastic so it will be OK."

Then she picked it up and said, "Look, I will show you its only plastic."

She threw it to the ground, expecting it to bounce. Unfortunately, it smashed into loads of pieces, as it was actually glass. At this point, Liz just stared at her and walked off, leaving Tina to deal with it.

Tina's way of dealing with it was to go to the assistant at

the till and tell her that there was a broken bauble on the floor that someone must have knocked off the shelf and she promptly ran off to catch up with Liz, who was horrified!

Liz marched her off to the coffee shop and made her sit there and not touch anything until they got on the flight. Tina got a coffee, so that kept her out of mischief until the flight was called, then, at last, Liz could drag her off towards the flight.

Almost home!

Well, the flight was rather uneventful. They had nice, comfy seats, and rather nice plane food for a change, but they were so shattered, as the time zone confused them and their body clocks.

The flight seemed endless, so they were glad to get off and walk again.

Tina's husband, Darran, had driven down to meet them and take them both home. They didn't have the energy to go for a train or any other method of getting home, so they were so pleased he was collecting them.

After catching up and a cuppa, they set off home. Neither of them could stay awake and, as both of them got travel sick in the back of a car, they had to decide who got the short straw.

Tina lost, so she curled up there and Liz did in the front seat. It must have been very boring for Darran, as they both slept most of the way home.

Darran had to drive a bit further on to drop Liz off at home. Their beds were beckoning!

Waking up in their own beds the next morning seemed like heaven, and it all seemed so long ago already – like a dream, or something that happened to somebody else, very weird.

No work until Monday, so at least they had three days to recover, which were desperately needed.

Lots of washing, shopping, and catching up with friends and family to be done before going back to the real world of work.

Liz felt shattered for the first week, but it took Tina around two weeks to start feeling normal again. This jet lag thing really hit them. They came to the conclusion that it was their age, or that was a reasonable excuse anyway.

They had set off with the plan of doing a tour taking them one thousand, one hundred and sixty miles, and the final mileage tally was one thousand five hundred.

If asked at the time 'Would they do this again?' 'NO WAY!' they both would have said.

It was certainly an adventure they felt they were lucky enough to experience and they didn't regret one minute of it, but do another one? Watch this space.

UPDATE ON TINA'S MUM - over the last few years, she had to endure a mastectomy and breast reconstruction surgery but is now in remission. It has been a hard slog, but she has come through it and is looking forward to the future.